CW00631949

with Local Tips
The author's special recommendations are
highlighted in yellow throughout this guide

There are five symbols to help you find your way around this guide:

Marco Polo's top recommendations – the best in each category

sites with a scenic view

places where the local people meet

places where young people get together

(102/A1)
pages and coordinates for the Road Atlas of South Africa
and the City Map of Johannesburg
(U/A1) *coordinates for the City Map of Cape Town inside back cover*
(O) *area not covered by maps*

MARCO ⊕ POLO

Travel guides and language guides in this series:

Algarve • Amsterdam • Australia/Sydney • Berlin • Brittany • California
Canada • Channel Islands • Costa Brava/Barcelona • Costa del Sol/Granada
Côte d'Azur • Crete • Cuba • Cyprus • Dominican Republic • Eastern Canada
Eastern USA • Florence • Florida • Gran Canaria • Greek Islands/Aegean
Ibiza • Ireland • Istanbul • Lanzarote • London • Mallorca • Malta • Mexico
New York • New Zealand • Normandy • Paris • Prague • Rhodes • Rome
Scotland • South Africa • Southwestern USA • Tenerife • Turkish Coast
Tuscany • Venice • Western Canada

*Marco Polo would be very interested to hear your
comments and suggestions. Please write to:*

North America:
Marco Polo North America
70 Bloor Street East
Oshawa, Ontario, Canada
(B) 905-436-2525

United Kingdom:
GeoCenter International Ltd
The Viables Centre
Harrow Way
Basingstoke, Hants RG22 4BJ

*Our authors have done their research very carefully, but should any errors or omissions
have occurred, the publisher cannot be held responsible for any injury, damage
or inconvenience suffered due to incorrect information in this guide*

Cover photograph: ZEFA/Landing
*Photos: Gartung (7, 37, 64, 74, 97); Kern (39, 42, 44, 47, 60, 70); Knipping (4);
Kress-Zorn (14, 17, 20, 22, 24); Lade: B & W (78), Dönit (67), Fiedler (11),
Welsh (34, 63); Mauritius: Hubatka (101), Reisel (28, 33), Ricatto (68), Vidler
(6, 9, 80, 86, 100); Schapowalow: Moser (55); Schuster: Gössler (69, 84);
Skupy (51); Skupy & Hartl (30, 58); Transglobe: Layda (82), Richardson (26)*

2nd revised edition 2000
© Mairs Geographischer Verlag, Ostfildern, Germany
Author: Dagmar Schumacher
Translator: Heather Stacey
English edition 2000: Gaia Text
Editorial director: Ferdinand Ranft
Chief editor: Marion Zorn
Cartography for the Road Atlas: © MapStudio, Cape Town
Design and layout: Thienhaus/Wippermann
Printed in Germany

CONTENTS

Discover South Africa!

Something for every taste: Fascinating cities next to the untouched world of the Kraal, barren steppes next to heavenly fertility, national parks next to beach life

South Africa is a holiday destination which has something to offer every traveller: glittering metropolises, lonely Zulu kraals, deserts, barren veld, subtropical forests, mountains as high as the Alps and breathtakingly beautiful waterfalls. Travel in luxury trains or covered wagons to see the 52 game and national parks and 3,000 kilometres of coastline with its wonderful beaches.

The sunny but temperate climate makes the southern tip of Africa an ideal holiday destination all year round. The period from October to April is especially enticing for visitors from the Northern Hemisphere since, as the days become shorter and snow and ice dampen the spirits in the North, summer comes to the Southern Hemisphere. This country at the southernmost point of the African continent covers an area of 1,221,042 km^2 and has a population of around 41 million. After the end of apartheid the country was reor-

ganised and divided into nine provinces: Northern Province, Mpumalanga, North West, Gauteng, Free State, KwaZulu-Natal, North Cape, West Cape and East Cape.

In 1488 the Portuguese seafarer, Bartholomeu Dias discovered the Cape of Good Hope. However, it was almost another 200 years before the first white settlers, under the leadership of Jan van Riebeeck, went ashore. They came here in order to establish a supply station for the Dutch East India Trading Company.

Yet the Cape region had already been inhabited for over a thousand years. At the time of the Portuguese discovery the area was populated by the Bushmen (San), a nomadic people, and the Hottentots, (related to both the Bushmen and the Bantu peoples) who lived by cattle breeding. The first settlers were paid a bonus if they married a Hottentot woman. The Dutch East India Company hoped that this would encourage the settlers to establish themselves. The descendants of the children of

The Cape of Good Hope is rounded every year by 20,000 ships

these mixed marriages were later classed by the apartheid regime as Coloureds, together with the mixed-race children of slave women and migrant workers from India.

During the early years of colonisation, the Dutch East India Company abducted slaves from Indonesia and West Africa and brought them to the Cape in an effort to alleviate the labour shortage. This had arisen because Jan von Riebeeck had forbidden the enslavement of the original inhabitants. The white settlers ('Boers'), who came from the Netherlands and Germany, were joined in 1688 by the first French settlers. These were 146 Huguenots who were forced to leave their native land because of religious persecution. It was they who first established the South African wine tradition.

At the end of the eighteenth century, the British attempted to seize the strategically valuable colony on the Cape and in 1814 they were eventually successful. This was a decisive moment for the organisation of the colony as the British accorded the 20,000 Hottentots the same rights as the 26,000 European settlers and freed the 30,000 slaves. Many of the Boer settlers could not come to terms with this new British colonial policy. They decided to set out as 'Voortrekkers' to explore inland. The Great Trek began in 1835 with covered wagons, pulled by oxen, which were pushed together at night to form a laager (barricade). It was the second major venture made by white settlers into the country's interior. They had already failed once, a century earlier, in the 'Frontier Wars' against the Xhosas. This time, however, they were victorious. During an attack by 12,000 Zulus, the Boers suffered no losses at all, while 3,000 of the Zulu warriors died.

The Voortrekkers repeatedly set up their own states which the British then always captured. Britain's drive towards the north was motivated not least by the rich gold and diamond deposits which were discovered

The Western Cape Province – famous world-wide for its wines

around this time. The clashes between the Boers and the British escalated and finally came to an end in 1899 after the three-year Boer War in which the British were victorious. Britain made the Boer Republics into British Crown colonies. At the end of May 1910, the constitution of the Union of South Africa came into force. The union of the four South African colonies remained part of the Commonwealth until 1961, when the Republic of South Africa was formed. From 1948 on, the country drifted into international obscurity. With growing concern the world followed the introduction of apartheid, the so-called separate development of the races. The country entered a blind alley and was only led out of it by Frederik Willem de Klerk.

De Klerk, who became head of government in 1989, decided to implement reforms. In February 1990, he released Nelson Mandela, the legendary leader of the ANC, who had spent a quarter of a century in prison. The release was made so that de Klerk could negotiate the future of South Africa with him. In 1991, he repealed the apartheid laws. In this way a basis of trust was established and the conditions created for all parties to work towards a peaceful handing over of power. Since 1996 South Africa has had a new constitution. In the first free and democratic elections in April 1994, Nelson Mandela was elected President.

Nelson Mandela describes South Africa as the rainbow nation and with good reason. South Africa comprises a great number of peoples and cultures, includ-

Xhosa woman wearing traditional headgear

ing the most populous groups of the Zulus, Xhosas and Sotho, the smaller ethnic groups such as the Tswana, Ndebele or Bushmen, as well as people of mixed race, Afrikaners (Boers) and British. In addition, there are immigrants from Europe. There are eleven official languages but English is spoken almost everywhere.

As in many holiday destinations in the Third World, there is also much poverty in South Africa which is made all the more glaring, since the wealth of the First World is often only a few kilometres away. The road from the Cape Town airport into the attractive city centre passes through vast slums where the government has only recently begun to invest large sums of money necessary for redevelopment.

One of the problems faced by the new South Africa (but also one of its opportunities) is the enormous size of the country. The most direct route from Johannesburg to Cape Town (via Bloemfontein or the diamond town of Kimberley) is about 1,600 kilometres. This is a ter-

History at a glance

1488
Dias sails round the Cape of Good Hope

1652
European settlers under Jan van Riebeeck set up the first supply station on the Cape

1658
The arrival of Asian and African slaves

1688
The arrival of the Huguenots

1779
The first of the 'Frontier Wars'

1795
British occupation of the Cape

1814
Rebellion of the Boers against the British administration

1815
Shaka becomes King of the Zulus

1820
5,000 British immigrants arrive in Port Elizabeth

1828
Free Coloureds granted the same rights as Whites

1834
Abolishment of slavery

1835
Beginning of the Great Trek

1838
Battle of Blood River between Boers and Zulus

1859
Arrival of Indian workers in Natal

1867
First diamonds discovered

1886
Gold discovered, foundation of Johannesburg

1902
End of the Second Anglo-Boer War

1910
The British colonies and the Boer Republics merge to form the Union of South Africa

1948
Election victory for the National Party: the beginning of official apartheid

1960
Resistance against the Pass Laws, 60 dead in Sharpeville

1961
Withdrawal from the Commonwealth

1983
Worst ANC bomb attack, 20 dead, 200 injured

1986
State of Emergency proclaimed. Relaxation of apartheid with the introduction of freedom of movement for Blacks

1990
Nelson Mandela released

1994
First free, democratic elections. Mandela becomes President

1996
Introduction of the new constitution

1999
Nelson Mandela retires as President. Thabo Mbeki wins elections for ANC

Johannesburg – known as the New York of Africa because of its skyline

rific distance, even though all the roads are excellent. A large part of the route goes through the arid Karoo scrubland, where it is possible to drive for hours without seeing another car. Because of this, it is advisable to have some provisions in the car, just in case. In the Karoo you pass the scattered gateways of the vast sheep farms. Many farmers offer reasonable overnight accommodation and breakfast.

After a journey from north to south, as you reach the top of the last mountain range which cuts the Cape off from the rest of South Africa, you might believe yourself to be in the Garden of Eden. The wine and fruit-cultivating areas and, in winter, the lush green fields of grain stretch out as far as the eye can see. In the distance, Cape Town, known as the Mother Town lies beside the sea at the foot of the Table Mountain and is one of South Africa's two capital cities. The Parliament sits here for six months and then, at the end of June, the government moves to the administrative capital, Pretoria. Cape Town is situated on a peninsula, the tip of which is the Cape of Good Hope. This is where the two seas which wash the shores of South Africa meet: the Indian Ocean in the east and the Atlantic in the west.

There are many attractions to a trip along the rougher West Coast but bathing in a warm sea is not one of them, however tempting it might look. Even on the hottest days, the water temperature rarely tops 17°C (63°F). Still, the natural surroundings are beautifully unspoilt. In fact, southern Africa is a wonderful place for bird lovers. Of the 27 orders of birds which exist globally, 22 are found here. The bird reserve at the Langebaan Lagoon is not to be missed. Going inland from the West Coast, the traveller reaches Namaqualand which, in spring (September/October), is transformed into a marvellous carpet of wild flowers.

The South African flora is incredibly rich and diverse; there are 20,000 different species of flowering plants. The national flower, protea, is known throughout the world, as is the jacaranda which, when in bloom bathes everything in a pale lilac light. It is especially beautiful in Pretoria during October.

For a seaside holiday, visitors should travel from Cape Town along the South and East Coast, coming first to the fishing villages of the Hermanus and Arniston on the Indian Ocean with their endless, inviting beaches. Here the spectacular *Garden Route* begins.

The superb road winds its way along the coast, bordered by mountain ranges for most of the way. Bathing resorts such as Knysna and Plettenberg Bay with their wonderful beaches, lagoons, lakes and estuaries make the region one of the most beautiful coastal holiday destinations in the world.

The Garden Route is 225 km long and, in spring, is the scene of an extravagant array of floral splendour. In the summer the region is a playground for watersports enthusiasts. For those without the time to travel to any of the large game parks, the area offers something similar. In the forests near Knysna (the largest in South Africa) there are elephants and to the north, inland at Oudtshoorn, is the centre for ostrich breeding. A number of farms can be visited and these huge birds observed at close quarters. Those brave enough can even have a ride.

Not far from Oudtshoorn are the Cango Caves, magnificent limestone caves which attract and impress thousands of visitors every year.

East London is the only river port in South Africa and it lies at the mouth of the Buffalo River. At the beginning of the last century it was the border town between the region populated by the European settlers and the ancestral land of the Xhosa people. In the Xhosa homelands of Transkei and Ciskei, there are many places with German names, such as Hamburg, Berlin, Potsdam, etc. They were founded by German settlers who landed here in 1857 and whose influence can still be felt today.

The region in South Africa which is most favoured by the weather is the province of KwaZulu-Natal, the kingdom of the Zulus. Tropical sunshine and frequent (often warm) rainfall means the land here is always green. The majority of the people of this province are Zulus who have a special place in the history of South Africa. They became famous, mainly through their leader, Shaka, whose warriors were admired for their courage, their determination and their pride, and were feared for their cruelty. In the Zulu lands, visitors can see the old battlefields.

The largest coastal city is Durban, a popular holiday destination. People in colourful summer clothes, saris and Zulu costume mingle on the streets. South African Indians account for approximately half the population of Durban. They are the descendants of the immigrant workers who were brought to Natal to work on the large sugar-cane plantations. Today, palaces decorated with columns still recall the fantastic wealth of the sugar barons. The subtropical climate makes bathing, sailing and surfing possible throughout the year.

Not very far from the hurly-burly of the city begins the Valley of a Thousand Hills. In peace and tranquillity, visitors can enjoy the indescribably beautiful views. From Pietermaritzburg, an excursion into the *Drakensberg Mountains* should not be missed. The massive mountain range is often known as the 'South African Alps'. One of the highest peaks is the *Mont aux Sources* (3,299 m).

A magnificent panorama is afforded by the 'Amphitheatre' in the Royal National Park which is formed by immense cliffs. In the mountains there is a wide range of country hotels. Walkers who explore the caves will find in many of them drawings by Bushmen.

The Berlin Falls in the Blyde River Canyon Nature Reserve

Natal, with its green, widely varying landscapes, starkly contrasts with the Orange Free State. This part of South Africa is rightly referred to as a 'wide, open land'. Here, as in the northern provinces, the only time it rains is in the summer. Then the countryside looks lush and green but in winter it is dreary — brownish yellow, dry and dusty.

However, this is when the African effect is at its most impressive. During the day the sun shines down from cloudless blue skies and in the evening, when within a very short space of time the temperatures drop by up to 20°C (68°F) to around freezing point or even below, you can sit round a cosily crackling fire. But beware! On evenings like this, even visitors from the Northern Hemisphere feel the cold. This is at least partly due to the altitude. The whole of the inland region of South Africa lies between 1,500 and 2,000 m above sea level.

Long ago, when the Voortrekkers, after a long and arduous journey, finally arrived in the former Transvaal, they believed that they had found the source of the Nile in a river which flowed northwards. This is how the little town of Nylstrom, near Warmbad got its name.

The two large cities in the north of the country are Johannesburg and Pretoria. They are actually so close that they will eventually merge into one. However, they could not be more different. Often known as the New York of South Africa, Johannesburg, with its glittering skyscrapers, is the country's most important industrial metropolis. This is where most of the banks and insurance companies and the stock market have their headquarters. English is the predominant language. In the languages of the Black South Africans, Johannesburg is called E'Goli, *City of Gold*. The city has gold to thank for its foundation and is truly built on gold. In the 1970s, two thirds of South Africa's export earnings came from gold and the figure today is still as high as forty per cent.

The centre of South Africa's economic power is surrounded by townships, the slums of the poor who are predominantly black. The most famous of these is Soweto.

In contrast to this, the seat of government in Pretoria has a much more tranquil image. It is mainly civil servants who live here. The city is situated at a height of 1,500 m, that is 400 m lower than Johannesburg, so the summers are warmer and the winters milder.

Further north, the landscape changes again. Here, as well, the climate is subtropical. The route leads through tea plantations and extensive plantation forests. The drive to Magoebaskloof is particularly impressive, winding through the forested mountain pass which is named after 'Magoebas', the leader of a gang which once hid out here. Of the many waterfalls in this area, the most impressive are the Debegeni Falls.

On the border with Mozambique lies the *Kruger National Park*, one of the largest game preserves in the world. It is not only the wealth of animals and birds to be found in the park which have

made it world-famous, but also the landscape. The vegetation is unique.

While Kruger National Park is the most well-known game preserve, it is by no means the only one. Game preservation has a long history. As early as 1656, the first decrees on hunting were issued. The first game reserve, which is now Kruger National Park, was established in 1898. Covering 21,086 km^2, it is very extensive indeed. Overnight accommodation is so highly sought-after that it is advisable to book twelve months in advance. Information on the National Parks is available from *South African National Parks (Tel. 012-343 19 91, Fax 343 09 05, e-mail: reservations @parks.sa.co.za)*

The Golden Gate Highlands Park in the Orange Free State is well worth a visit. Here antelopes and birds live in beautiful, undisturbed natural surroundings. The Mountain Zebra National Park was established for the preservation of the mountain zebras. In the Kalahari Gemsbok Park, lions can still be seen and in the Tsitsikamma Park, there are crocodiles and other aquatic animals.

In addition, there is the Umfolozi Game Reserve in Natal which is famous for its rhinoceroses. Most of the parks can easily be driven through by car.

Altogether, South Africa is the ideal country for a driving holiday. The cost of hiring a car, especially on the weekend and for longer periods, is very reasonable. The roads are also good, even those which are not made up. There are only a few places, in the former Homelands, where the roads leave something to be desired. This is due to decades of neglect. However, they are now gradually being improved. The South Africans drive on the left. The majority of service stations do not accept credit cards so it is advisable always to carry cash.

When planning a driving holiday, it is important to bear in mind that it gets dark much earlier in South Africa than, for example, in Europe. Even in summer, night falls between seven and eight and in winter dusk is an hour earlier. Drivers are strongly advised to keep to the speed limits, as fines are steep. The limits are 60 km/h in urban areas, 100 km/h on secondary roads and 120 km/h on the highways.

Those who do not wish to drive themselves, can take advantage of the wide variety of bus trips on offer. The benefit here is that you can rely on having a well-informed guide. Information is available from *Satour, Tel. 012-347 06 00, Fax 012/45 48 89, e-mail: satour@is.co.za*

In the holiday paradise of South Africa, there is a choice of 1,300 hotels which meet the whole range of requirements at reasonable prices. They are divided into five different categories, from one to five stars, whereby one star denotes a satisfactory hotel and the five-star hotels are comparable with the best in the world. Plenty of private accommodation is also available (B & B), giving visitors an insight into the life of South African people. *Central reservation bureau 011/880 34 14, Fax 788 48 02, e-mail: places@aztec.co.za*

South Africa can be divided roughly into two climatic zones:

on the one hand, the coastal belt and the Cape and, on the other, the inland region. In Cape Town and its hinterland, summer is dry and sunny. Rainfall is generally restricted to the winter months. The hottest month is February, with average temperatures of 27°C (81°F), while the coolest time is in July, with daytime temperatures of around 15°C (59°F).

The rest of the country, the high inland plateau, the hilly country of Natal and the lowveld in the north, are summer rain areas. The rainy season is between September and April, often with thunderstorms in the late afternoon. In Johannesburg, the warmest time is in January, with average temperatures of 26°C (79°F), and the coldest in July, with an average temperature of 17°C (63°F). The hottest weather is experienced in the area around Kimberley and Upington: 33°C (91°F) in January.

South Africa has something to offer in all seasons. Game parks are best visited in the winter because the grass is shorter then. Durban is the place to go for a sun tan. The best months in Cape Town and for the drive along the Garden Route are March, April and May. During the holiday season, in December and January, everywhere along the coast is likely to be crowded.

Anyone who decides to go to South Africa for Christmas instead of spending it at home should be sure to book a hotel room in good time.

South Africa advertises itself with the slogan 'A world in one country'. You'll soon discover that this is no exaggeration.

From the Afrikaners to the Zulus

Living in the rainbow nation after the years of apartheid.
Black and white – united and full of hope for the future

Afrikaners

The Boers are the descendants of the Dutch and German settlers of whom a large proportion started out as farmers (Boer translates as 'farmer'). They call themselves Afrikaners to emphasise the fact that they are white inhabitants of Africa. They speak *Afrikaans,* a mixture of Dutch and German which also includes some French, Malay and Zulu and a few Hottentot words. The Afrikaners are very proud of their language which finds expression in a rich and diverse literature. Because of their Calvinist faith, they are the most united section of the white population. From 1948 to 1994, through the National Party, they formed the government of the country which was responsible for introducing the apartheid system. Economic sanctions, global isolation and the bloody and courageous resistance within South Africa itself forced the then President, Frede-

With six million people, the Zulus are the largest population group in South Africa

rik Willem de Klerk, to turn away from this unjust system in 1990. From 1994 until the middle of 1996, the National Party still formed part of the first democratically elected government.

ANC

Founded in 1912 and banned in 1960, the African National Congress fought successfully in a liberation war lasting decades against control by the white minority. The ANC is now the strongest party in the country. Until 1999 it was led by Nelson Mandela, the Nobel Peace Prize winner, who became President in 1994. Thabo Mbeki assumed leadership after the 1999 elections.

Apartheid

The word comes from the Afrikaans and means 'segregation'; the legal segregation and unequal legal position of people in all areas of life on the basis of the colour of their skin. This racist doctrine was an attempt by the whites, especially by the Boer minority, to prevent the numerically far superior black population of South Africa from gaining power. From 1948, this discriminatory dogma, which even boasted a theological underpinning, enforced a jumble of Race Laws. The segregation of all people according to the colour of their skin, together with the establishment of ten so-called *Homelands,* created a situation of endless misery and poverty for the non-whites.

Bushmen

The Bushmen (San), together with the Hottentots, are the original inhabitants of South Africa. They are small-statured people who have a yellowish-brown skin and slanting eyes. There are only a few of them left today, as they were almost completely wiped out by the Boers. The small remaining populations of this nomadic people today still live in the manner of their forebears thousands of years ago. They build huts from bush and sticks above a small hollow in the sand. The Bushmen are shy and freedom-loving people and, over the course of the last few centuries, as more and more people came, they have retreated into isolated, fairly infertile regions of southern Africa. They are so well-adapted to their environment that, even in the desert, they can survive for several days without food or water. Rock paintings which can be found all over the country portray the tradition of these people with their ancient, cheerful culture. It is hard to say from what time the oldest cave paintings date, but one of their later works, a painting in the Drakensberg Mountains, shows men with white faces who are pictured approaching on horseback. They are wearing hats and are armed with rifles.

Coloureds

The origins of the mixed-race peoples of South Africa can be traced back to 1652. This was the year when the first white settlers arrived. Coloureds are the descendants of marriages between Europeans and Hottentots, Bushmen, Asian and black women. They live mostly in Cape Town and the Cape provinces. Almost all the people working in the vineyards are coloureds, for example. During apartheid, the 'Coloured' South Africans were treated very badly. A large, undeveloped plot of land in the middle of Cape Town is all that remains today of District Six, the area where the coloureds formerly lived. And even today it is still a source of deep bitterness.

The coloureds lived in this part of the town, which was full of slums but also of *joie de vivre,* until the middle of the 1960s. Then, in the course of apartheid policy, all the buildings (with the exception of the churches) were razed to the ground. Cape Town was to become white. The coloureds have still neither forgotten nor forgiven this action and even now, in the new South Africa, the reconstruction of the area has begun only hesitantly.

Television

State television was not introduced in South Africa until 1976. When it finally arrived, however, it was top quality. Three channels broadcast programmes in nine different languages. English programmes are shown on all channels. The private channel, M-Net, mainly broadcasts feature films and sport in English. Most hotels are equipped with the special decoder which is necessary in order to receive M-Net. A number of other private TV stations began broadcasting in 1999.

Flora and fauna

There is probably no place else in the world which can boast such a wealth of flora. The varying climatic conditions in the different regions give rise to the diverse range of plants. For example, there are 400 different varieties of the South African national flower, the protea. The country's floral splendour can best be admired in the many wild flower and botanical gardens. South Africa's nature reserves are home to a wide variety of both flora and fauna: a plethora of plant species and an overwhelming number of animals.

In terms of fauna, South Africa has everything: from the dwarf shrew, which only weighs ten grams, right up to the elephant, which can weigh as much as six tonnes. Being separated by nothing more than a car windscreen from a lion in its natural surroundings, or standing opposite a herd of elephants, are unforgettable experiences. Of the 830 species of birds, a large number spend the winter in South Africa. So it is not at all unusual, during the European winter months, to see hundreds of storks standing in a field.

Homelands

The so-called Homelands were an attempt by the government, in the name of apartheid, to create ten independent states for the black population. Thus, the large, remaining part of South Africa was left free for settlement by the whites. The Homelands were established in the areas which had been inhabited historically by different black peoples. Thus, to give just a few examples, the Xhosa were given Transkei and Ciskei, the Zulus were all supposed to live in Kwa-Zulu and the Tswana were given Bophuthatswana. These reservations accounted for 13 per cent of the land area but eighty per cent of the population of South Africa lived in them. As a result, the Homelands were completely overpopulated. Mainly, it was elderly people, women and children who lived there. The family breadwinners were employed outside the Homelands as migrant workers, in industry or

Protea, the national flower

agriculture, wherever white South Africa could make use of them. Families were torn apart, since fathers came home perhaps once a year, if at all. The misery and poverty were immense. Today, the Homelands are again part of South Africa but it will be some time before the legacy of apartheid is no longer visible.

Hottentots

When Jan van Riebeeck and his settlers arrived in 1652, the Hottentots were cattle-rearers and gatherers who were living in the Cape in modest prosperity. Like the Bushmen, the Hottentots belong to the Khoisan peoples. They carried loads on their backs and not, like other black African peoples, on their heads. The Hottentots were of medium height, their skin colour was pale brown and they had quite pronounced hips. Their 10,000 year history ended with the arrival of the Boers who almost completely wiped out these original inhabitants of the Cape. The few who survived were soon absorbed into other groups. Even today, remnants of the Hottentot language still survive in Afrikaans.

Indaba

This term was originally only used for the meetings of the Zulu chieftains. Now, however, it is also used to refer to political and other meetings. For example, South Africa's largest trade fair is called Indaba.

Indians

The Indians are the smallest population group in South Africa. Their forebears came to Natal in the middle of the 19th century to work in the plantations of the sugar barons. The majority of them live in Durban and in KwaZulu-Natal. Some are Hindu and some Muslim. The Indians were also discriminated against during apartheid.

Mandela

In 1990, after more than 25 years in prison, Nelson Mandela, by then over seventy years old, was released. A lawyer, who was originally sentenced to life imprisonment for activities which were hostile to the state, sabotage and the dissemination of communist ideas, Mandela was immediately transformed into the most important leading political figure in South Africa. In April 1994, after the first free and democratic elections, he became President. On Nelson Mandela's release from prison, the well-known South African writer, Breyten Breytenbach, wrote 'He went in as an activist and came out as a myth... Nelson Mandela opened a door'.

And so it came to pass. The peaceful transformation of the country is due to a large extent to Mandela, who became a unifying figure for South Africans of all colours.

Museums

There are museums even in the smallest towns. It may be due to the relatively short history of the country that South Africans have such a predilection for museums. Europeans, spoilt by their much longer history, may not fully appreciate the care and attention which has been put into creating many of these collections.

Muti

This is the magical cure of the medicine men and natural healers, who are also known as sangomas. In mysterious shops in Johannesburg and Pretoria, you can get expert advice when buying muti or have your future read from bones thrown onto the floor. Sangomas enjoy an excellent reputation. Many black people will go to the doctor and then, to be on the safe side, to the medicine man or woman as well. In Soweto, there are over 5,000 sangomas.

National Party

The overwhelmingly Afrikaans-speaking National Party ruled South Africa from 1948. Not only did it establish and support the prosperity of its white voters, it was also responsible for writing the grossly unjust apartheid system into the statute books. Racial segregation reached its peak in the 1960s under the 'Father of Apartheid', the Dutch-born Hendrik Verwoerd.

Shebeens

This is the name given to the pubs and clubs in the Black townships. The atmosphere is almost always explosive, especially in the evenings and on the weekends. The drinks are not always cold (due to rapid sales), but this is made up for by the music which is amazing. It is advisable to invite a guide who knows his way around.

Sports

It is no surprise that the inhabitants of such a sun-blessed land are such ardent sportsmen and women. The South Africans en-joy all manner of sports. In summer, national interest is mainly focused on cricket, in winter on rugby. There are over 400 golf courses where tourists are welcome to play, on payment of a 'Visitor Fee'. Golf buggies are available and, at the larger courses, clubs, etc., can be hired. The Drakensberg Mountains and the hills of the Cape Provinces are particularly good for hiking and hill walking. Bloemfontein is the most popular place for gliding. In most places on the coast, visitors can enjoy surfing, diving, sailing, deep sea fishing and wind surfing. Many hotels have tennis courts and there is hardly a hostel without a swimming pool.

Townships

This is the term used to describe the suburbs. During the apartheid regime, there was a law which segregated residential areas according to skin colour. Each town or city had white, coloured or Indian and black areas, even though, in the cities, the distinctions between them became increasingly blurred. The word township is now used in reference to the many, enormous non-white suburbs. They are becoming noticeably run down, not least because more people arrive every day from the rural areas, hoping to find work in the towns. Barely half of all South Africans live in proper houses. The other half attempt to build themselves some kind of shelter out of wood, plastic sacks and tin sheets. Anyone who does have a roof over their heads sublets to those less fortunate. It is not unusual for ten people to sleep in a tiny room.

Nearly three million blacks are undernourished. More than a third of them are children under five years old. As anywhere in the Third World, a visit to the poorer residential areas should be undertaken with caution. Anyone who feels they have to see the poverty for themselves can go on an organised bus trip around Soweto, near Johannesburg.

Soweto: The new government has been able to do little so far about the conditions in which many blacks live

Wildlife

For visitors who are interested in the animal kingdom, South Africa is a paradise. The country's game reserves boast a larger number of different species than almost anywhere else in the world. There are 17 National Parks in South Africa which altogether cover an area of 3.2 million hectares. In addition, there are also all the nature reserves run by the provinces and countless private game parks. Most of them are situated in the summer rain areas. The lush vegetation can make it difficult to watch the animals during the summer months, so it is best to visit in the dry winter, from May to September. The animals are at their most active just before dawn and shortly before sunset. These factors should be taken into account when planning a safari.

Economy

Due to the deposits of gold, diamonds and other minerals, mining is one of the most important branches of industry in South Africa. Besides agriculture, it also offers the most jobs. Since 1886, South Africa has been the largest gold producer in the world, supplying over 50 per cent of global demand, although there is now a downwards trend. The gold market is periodically rocked by crises. The most up-to-date methods are used for the extraction of gold which is essential, especially in the case of very deep mines. The precious metal is not found as nuggets of gold, but rather as a very fine gold dust which runs through solid rock in the form of veins. Sometimes the galleries and tunnels are over 4,000 metres below the ground. All the gold mines are owned by firms which make up the Chamber of Mines in Johannesburg.

South Africa is also one of the largest diamond producers in the world. In fact, there are few minerals which are not to be found here. In some cases, for example the titanium-rich magnetic rock vanadium, South Africa has the monopoly on extraction.

Agriculture, with its vine and cereal cultivation and cattle and sheep rearing, may not be so significant in terms of exports, but it is certainly a very important employer.

Each year, 1.2 million fish are caught in the seas around the Cape. 90 per cent are sold abroad. Crayfish, in particular, are served up in gourmet restaurants and at the finest buffets all over the world.

Tourism is a relatively new branch of the economy, but it is already the third largest source of foreign exchange. South Africa looks forward to continuing growth in this area, since, owing to the exchange rate, it is an attractive holiday destination for visitors from abroad.

Xhosa

Contrary to the 'white' version of history formerly written in South Africa, the Xhosa tribes lived in the areas now known as Transkei and Ciskei as long ago as the 15th century. The first descriptions were written by ship-wrecked sailors of that time. A Portuguese journalist who was stranded in the Xhosa area in 1635 described them thus: 'The men in this land are slim and upright, tall and handsome. They are capable of enduring hunger and cold and they work hard. They live for 200 years and remain healthy throughout their lives and retain all their teeth.' When travelling through these rural areas today, the women can often be seen sitting in front of their round huts, with a long pipe, wearing their traditional tribal dress of elaborately embroidered cloth. They often paint their faces and the faces of their children white which was probably originally intended to protect them from the sun. This aspect of their traditions is still followed by many Xhosa women even in the towns.

Zulus

With over six million people, the Zulus are the largest population group in South Africa. Their traditional home is the Kingdom of Zululand in Natal. They are famous for their war-like history. Even today, supporters of the largely Zulu Inkatha party still get into fights with ANC members. At the beginning of the last century especially, the Zulus were feared throughout the whole region. At that time they were ruled by King Shaka who was a military genius. There are many legends about him which still survive. His army was made up of 50,000 men and 10,000 women. His kingdom extended along the Tugela River and included most of the area which is now known as Natal. Shaka is remembered today as a great but also brutal leader. Whenever he won a victory against another tribe, he immediately had the chieftains, their wives and children murdered. Eventually his bloodthirstiness led Shaka's brother, Dingaan, to murder him and seize power himself. He led the Zulu army against the Boers and later against the British colonial troops. In 1872, after the final battle in Ulundi, the victorious British divided the kingdom which had been established by Shaka into 13 separate areas, each with its own chieftain.

From exquisite wines to ethnic specialities

*Asian, Indian, European and Afrikaans cuisine
with wonderful South African wines –
a treat for the most discerning connoisseurs*

Food

There is no authentic South African cuisine. Different specialities are served in different areas. Around the Cape the influence of Malayan cooking is particularly strong, for example in *babotie,* a pie made from minced lamb with curry and potatoes, and *bredies,* a sort of vegetable stew. Tomato bredie is especially to be recommended. The Indians in Natal like to serve hot curry and chutney dishes. Then there are *samoosas*, small triangular pastry envelopes which are filled with vegetable or meat curry.

The Afrikaners love their *braai,* a barbecue, which is often memorable more for its conviviality than for its culinary delights. Excellent steaks and *boerewors,* a well-spiced sausage, are

*Popular refreshment: Sorghum beer —
made in South Africa*

cooked on the grill. *Sosaties* are pieces of lamb with dried fruits, apple rings and tomatoes which are put on skewers and are also prepared on the barbecue. They are served with *stywe pap,* a sort of porridge made of maize and cooked until it is almost completely dried out. A particularly Afrikaner way of eating the *pap* is to roll it into a ball in your hands and dip it in a sauce, before eating it with the sausage. On weekends, South Africa is enveloped in the smell of countless braai parties. It is a popular activity: the men stand around the fire, a bottle of beer in their hands, while the women sit at the table and discuss the problems of day to day life. For dessert *koeksisters* are very popular. These are sweet biscuits which are woven into a plait.

Most restaurants serve a wide selection of fish which, in coastal areas at least, is guaranteed to be freshly caught. The *crayfish* is a cross between lobster and crawfish. Compared to prices in Europe, this delicacy is available fairly cheaply in South Africa. However, before ordering crayfish, it is advisable to ask whether it is fresh, rather than frozen, as it tastes much better fresh. In addition, ask to be shown the size of the fish! *Kingklip* is a fish which is highly prized by the South Africans. The meat is white and firm and it generally tends to be served filleted. *Snoek* is a type of barracuda which has a strong flavour and is fairly fatty. It is usually sold smoked, with herbs or whole pepper corns. *Perlemoen*, which is also known as *abalone*, is a mussel, about the size of a fist, which is found in large numbers in the Atlantic Ocean.

The range of fruit and vegetables available is very wide and of excellent quality. Most produce is grown outdoors which significantly affects the smell and flavour. Mushrooms are the only exception. As in supermarkets everywhere, they tend to be fairly pale and insipid. In South Africa asparagus is almost always green because cultivation of the white variety has only recently begun. Grapes, melons and apples are particularly recommended. Most common kinds of fruit and vegetables are available, with a couple of unusual additions, such as *Cape gooseberries*, which are unique to the Cape. These small, yellow fruits are used mainly in cakes and preserves. In addition, from May onwards *waterblommetjies* can often be found growing on ponds. The flowers of these water plants look rather like waterlilies and are only found on the Cape. They are usually used in a lamb stew.

Another South African speciality is *biltong*. Don't be put off by its appearance. Biltong is made from pieces of raw meat, usually beef, game or ostrich, which are salted, spiced and then dried in the open air. It is actually very tasty. Biltong is

Sweet, juicy fruit is available all year round from all the markets

sold in special shops as well as butcher shops and supermarkets. The dried, filleted pieces of meat are hung up on display and the customer chooses one which is then cut up into small pieces using a special machine. Toothpicks are included!

Drink

The tap water is quite safe to drink everywhere. South Africa has among the best quality drinking water in the world. Consequently, mineral water has only become fashionable in recent years. Because of the high temperatures, South Africans order a glass of iced water with every meal. The most popular drink amongst the black population is beer, while white South Africans enjoy brandy and coke. Many people also like to drink spirits. Gin, rum, vodka and whisky are popular and there are many types of schnapps which are produced in South Africa, or at least bottled here. Although wine has been produced for 300 years, the South Africans have only really developed a taste for it over the last fifteen years. South African wines are excellent and the Cape area is a paradise for wine connoisseurs. The grapes grow in ideal conditions, kissed by the sun.

For those who begin their trip at the Cape, the best thing to do is to go on the Franschhoek, Stellenbosch, Paarl or Constantia wine routes. Wine tastings provide a great opportunity for identifying the best table wines for the rest of the trip. Here are a few recommendations: *Meerlust, De Wetshof Klein Constantia, Blaauwklippen, Boschendal, Le Bonheur, L'Ormarins, Nederburg, Rustenberg, Simonsig* and *Stellenryck* produce excellent red and white wines.

The local coffee may not always taste good to visitors who come here from abroad. However, in many restaurants espressos and cappuccinos are often served also. It is certainly well worth trying *rooibos tea,* which is only found in South Africa. It is made from a fruit which is quite similar to the rose hip. The only place it grows is near Clanwilliam on the West Coast.

Restaurants

The choice of restaurants is immense, especially in the larger towns and holiday resorts. The cuisine is international, since there is hardly a nationality which is not represented in South Africa. Some restaurants, particularly smaller ones, tend to be unlicensed. There is also a difference between a full licence and a licence which just permits the sale of wine and beer. If a restaurant displays a sign which says it is *unlicensed*, then diners are free to bring along their own alcoholic drinks.

There are *bottle stores* all over the place, where alcohol can be purchased. Most supermarkets do not sell alcohol. You will usually be told whether or not the restaurant is licensed when you reserve your table. It should be noted that it is always advisable to reserve a table, especially when dining in the larger towns and cities. It is also important to be aware that in certain restaurants and hotels, especially in the evening, diners are expected to dress smartly.

Beads and jewellery tell their own tales

*A treasure-trove of unusual handicrafts,
diamonds and ostrich leather*

Hand-crafted objects are particularly popular as souvenirs. Consequently, South Africa is a wonderful place for souvenirs with a wide variety of things to choose from, including decorative clothing, attractive jewellery and handicrafts, such as carvings and items made from beads. The bead work is fascinating – the beads speak their own language and are used to convey messages. For example, the Zulus and Xhosas send love letters which are little mats made from beads and hung on safety pins.

The choice of souvenirs is very extensive and there is only room here for a few tips about the particular skills of different sections of the population. The Zulus make small cloth dolls decorated with beads, birds from pine cones and *calabash*, bowls made from gourds and covered with beads. *Inxhili*, traditional white

The market in front of the town hall in Cape Town

and orange bags, decorated with beads and buttons, are typically made by the Xhosa, as is the *isibinquo*, a three-quarter-length decorative skirt with a matching top called a *gilet*. Very attractive table cloths are also made in this style. The long pipe decorated with beads is known as an *inquawe*. The Ndebele are famous for their loincloths which are worn by both men and women. The cloths vary in size. Different beadwork patterns on goat skin show whether or not a woman is married and, in the case of a youth, whether he has already gone through the masculinity ritual. Dolls up to a metre in height and embroidered with beads are meant to portray fertility and masculinity.

Nyoka is the name given by the Ndebele to the bride's headdress. The bead jewellery, bangles and chains are highly colourful and it is well worth trying to find an opportunity to watch some of these items being made.

27

The Ndebele women are famous for their painting and embroidered bead work

The souvenirs are sold on the streets and in lots of tourist shops. On weekends there are flea markets in all the larger towns where the vendors demonstrate their imagination and creativity. Many small handicraft items are fashioned in workshops in the poorer areas. Anyone with an interest in antiques and junk should definitely have a look round here, as it is sometimes possible to find quite a bargain.

Children from the black townships often sell handicraft items on the street corners. They make models of things such as windmills, cars and bicycles from wire and metal. This form of art has been developed as a result of the children's poverty: if they want toys, they have to make them for themselves.

Since the end of apartheid, more and more handicraft items, especially wooden articles, are being brought into South Africa from other African countries. They are sold on street corners and at flea markets. In the countries where they come from, there are regular mass production lines. It is wise, therefore, to be cautious, when offered an expensive 'antique' wooden carving from Zimbabwe, for example. Anyone who wishes to buy such items would be better going to an art gallery.

The *curio shops* are something between a street stall and an art shop. They are roughly comparable to the craft shops found in Europe and elsewhere.

Many visitors expect jewellery to be cheaper in South Africa, the land of gold and diamonds. This is true, but only to a certain extent. The price of gold and precious stones is, in South Africa as in other countries, controlled by the international market. Nevertheless, it may well be worth buying jewellery, if it is produced in South Africa, since wages are much lower here. In addition, the quality of the pieces produced is excellent. However, visitors are advised only to buy jewellery in a proper shop run by a Master Goldsmith.

It is also important to be wary of imported jewellery, since an 85 per cent luxury and import tax is added to the price. Diamonds in the top colours and coloured stones are often better value as they are not so popular with South African women.

VAT (value added tax) at a rate of 14 per cent can be refunded at the airport to tourists who can produce the receipt and the item purchased. This is the case for anything worth more than 250 Rand. However, anyone who intends to take advantage of this option should allow for an extra hour at the airport.

Since South Africa is *the* ostrich-farming country, it is well worth buying items made from the scarred leather of these huge birds. There is a very wide choice of handbags, brief cases, suitcases, purses and even shoes. Unfortunately, these items are no longer as cheap as they once were, since the popularity of ostrich leather has increased immensely. Nevertheless, by comparing prices, it is still possible to find a bargain. It is important to be aware when buying ostrich leather that items made without using the pimply leather are much cheaper. This is because the smoother material comes from the legs of the ostrich and is considered to be less valuable.

South Africa is a paradise for wine connoisseurs. This is not only on account of the quality, but also because of the price. Even the best wines rarely cost more than 30 R a bottle. A decent wine can be bought for 7.50 R. For real enthusiasts it is worth buying a wine guide, available from all stationers. Almost all the wine-growing estates offer wine tasting sessions and also arrange for the wine to be transported home for you.

For those who find the idea of driving about from estate to estate and along the various wine routes too laborious, there are plenty of wine shops in Cape Town where the whole range of South African wines is available. Sending wine home from here is also usually fairly straightforward. The following shops are highly recommended: *Caroline's Fine Wine Cellar; 15 Long St.; Tel. 021/419-89 84,* or *Enoteca; Heritage Sq.; Tel. 021/24 91 67.* The huge vine in front of this shop is said to be the oldest in South Africa.

The kiosks which are to be found throughout the towns and in every village are very handy. They call themselves *cafés* and open at six o'clock in the morning and seldom close before midnight. They sell newspapers, food, cigarettes, sweets, soft drinks and much more. There is often an adjoining snack bar, too.

Carnivals, street parties and festivals

The colourful medley of folklore, floral splendour, music and dance make South African festivals an unforgettable experience

PUBLIC HOLIDAYS

1 January *New Year's Day*
21 March *Human Rights Day*
27 April *Freedom Day*
16 June *Youth Day*
9 August *National Women's Day*
24 September *Heritage Day*
16 December *Day of Reconciliation*
When any of these holidays fall on a Sunday, then the following Monday is a public holiday.

RELIGIOUS HOLIDAYS

Around three quarters of all South Africans belong to one of the Christian churches. So Christmas, Easter and Ascension Day are holidays throughout the country. Other holidays tend only to be celebrated by members of the respective religions. In Cape Town and Johannesburg, for example, many of the shops are closed for Jewish festi-

Tribal dancing is an old tradition at many festivals

vals. South Africans of Malayan origin are mostly Muslim and the Indians in Natal mostly Hindu.

FESTIVALS & LOCAL EVENTS

1–7 January
★*Coon Carnival in Cape Town:*
Street carnival organised by the Coloureds. Brightly dressed, they process through the streets in groups, dancing and playing stringed instruments and saxophones. The high point is a competition in the Green Point Stadium to decide which is the best band. *Information: Tel. 021/397-6429*

Last week in March
Klein Karoo National Arts Festival:
This cultural festival takes place in Oudtshoorn, the capital of ostrich leather production. Here lots of shows are performed in Afrikaans. Then there is the art market with a wide selection of handicraft items. *Information: Tel. 044/27 27 77*

31

Last weekend in March
Durban Fiesta and Harbour Festival: Big city and harbour festival in Durban with barbecues on the beaches.

March/April
Rand Easter Show in Johannesburg: Largest consumer trade fair in the country. Plenty of entertainment. *Information: Tel. 011/494 91 11*

First week in April
Castle Lite Two Ocean Marathon: Well over 10,000 runners take part in this race across the Cape Peninsula between the Atlantic and Indian Oceans. *Information: Tel. 021/61 94 07*

Last weekend in May
Royal Show in Pietermaritzburg: An amazing combination of agricultural show, art sale and party. *Information: Tel. 033/45 62 74*

31 May
Comrades Marathon: A race from Pietermaritzburg to Durban which takes place every year.

Mid June
Zululand Show: Big Zulu show in Eshowe which is accompanied by an agricultural exhibition.

Last week of June/ first week of July
Standard Bank National Arts Festival in Grahamstown: During the two weeks of the festival this sleepy little university town is transformed into an enormous arts arena. A must for culture enthusiasts. Each day is packed with theatre, films and music. All of South Africa's most important exhibitions are shown here. *Information: Tel. 0466/22 71 15*

First weekend in July
Durban July: The high point of the horse racing season at the Greyville racetrack in Durban.

First week in July
Knysna Oyster Festival: All the events here are centred around oysters. For example, there is an oyster cooking competition with an oyster eating competition the next day. Plus lots of sporting events.

Nearest Sunday to 14 July
Bastille Day in Franschhoek: The day when the wine-growers and restaurant owners commemorate the founders of the town. A festival with the best dishes and wines in the area.

Nearest weekend to 25 July
Shembefest: Zulu religious festival with tribal dances in *Ekupakuneni* near Durban.

Last weekend in July
★ *Kimberley Steam Festival:* A must for steam engine enthusiasts. During the festival the town demonstrates its impressive collection of old steam locomotives.

August to October
★ *Wild flowers blooming in Namaqualand:* During this period over 2,600 plant varieties bloom in the floral paradise of the West Coast of the Cape. They form a carpet of flowers which stretches for kilometres in all directions. Each town holds its own Flower Festival. (See also Route 2 'A trip into floral wonderland', p. 90). *Information from Flowerline; Tel. 021/418 37 05*

MARCO POLO SELECTION: FESTIVALS

1 **Coon Carnival in Cape Town**
The music festival organised by the coloureds (page 31)

2 **Steam Festival in Kimberley**
Vintage steam engine show (page 32)

3 **Wild flowers in bloom Namaqualand**
From August to October, celebrations in every town on the West Coast (page 32)

4 **Whale Festival in Hermanus**
A festival to celebrate the mating season of the whales (page 33)

Last weekend in September
★ *Whale Festival in Hermanus:* Whales frequent the coast of the Indian Ocean between Plettenberg Bay and Hermanus from June to November. They come in order to mate and to give birth to their young. The festival weekend is devoted entirely to the whales. *Information: Tel. 0283/217 85*

Last Tuesday in September until the following Saturday
Cape Times Waterfront Wine Festival in Cape Town: The largest public wine festival in South Africa. Almost every region and every large wine-growing estate is represented. The 22.50 R entry fee entitles the visitor to a wine glass and then tasting is unlimited.

Third week in October
Bloemfontein Rose Festival: With this festival the Rose City truly lives up to its name.

Last Wednesday to Saturday in October
Stellenbosch Food and Wine Festival: A great opportunity to taste under one roof all the wines which come from the area around Stellenbosch.

A Zulu at the Durban Fiesta

October
Jacaranda Carnival: When the jacaranda trees bloom, Pretoria celebrates with a street party.

December
1 Million Golf Tournament: The top players in the world are invited to Sun City/Lost City.

Third week in December
❖ *Rothmans Week:* This sailing regatta from Cape Town to Saldanha is the largest in South Africa.

A peninsula full of contrasts

Nowhere else in South Africa are there charming bays, rich wine-growing country, mighty mountain ranges and barren deserts in such close proximity

The Cape Provinces account for around 60 per cent of the land area and boast the most contrasting landscapes in South Africa. There is plenty to see in this wonderful region ranging from floral paradises to desert.

The Cape Peninsula is 51 km long and at no point is it wider than 16 km. With its mountain ranges, bordered on both sides by oceans,

Cape Town city centre at the foot of Table Mountain

the Peninsula alone makes a trip to South Africa worthwhile. Cape Town, with its exclusive suburbs and the harbour in Table Bay, is breathtakingly beautiful. Yet the rest of the Peninsula is in no way less impressive, with its little fishing villages, lovely coastal roads, wonderful beaches and nature reserves and, at the southern tip, the Cape of Good Hope which was described by Sir Francis Drake as, 'the fairest Cape we saw in the whole circumference of the earth'.

Hotel and restaurant prices

Hotels

Category 1: over 150 R
Category 2: 120–150 R
Category 3: under 120 R
Based on the price of a double room for one person for one night with breakfast.

Restaurants

Category 1: over 75 R
Category 2: 45–75 R
Category 3: under 45 R
These prices are based on a meal with a starter, main course and dessert, including drinks.

Important abbreviations

Ass.	Association	**Sq.**	Square
St.	Street	**Dr.**	Drive
Rd.	Road	**Ave.**	Avenue

South Africa's wine-producing country begins in the northern suburbs of Cape Town, with an area of country mansions built in the Cape Dutch style, surrounded by vineyards. Grapes have been cultivated here for over 300 years.

The Cape Provinces include large tracts of the arid *Karoo* scrubland. Anyone who enjoys solitude will love this landscape. There is something fascinating about the combination of silence, sheer vastness and light. Coming from the Cape, this is where visitors for the first time feel that they are in Africa. The Karoo is an expanse of semi-desert covered with small bushes and used for grazing sheep. Karoo lamb has a distinctive taste.

On the Indian Ocean side, the Cape is luxuriantly green and fertile. The abundance of water here gives rise to the name of the famous *Garden Route.* The name does not mean that there are gardens arranged one after the other. The Garden Route describes a stretch of particularly beautiful landscape. If you come from the arid Karoo through the Swartberg Pass and suddenly see this garden landscape stretching out before you, there really is no better description for it. The most attractive section of the coastal road is between Mossel Bay and the Storms River Mouth, a distance of 225 km in all. The first Europeans in South African history landed at Mossel Bay. After Bartholomeu Dias had rounded the Cape of Good Hope, he dropped anchor here so that he could replenish his water stocks. He did find a water source in

MARCO POLO SELECTION: CAPE PROVINCES

1 Table Mountain
Visitors glide to the top of the over 1,000-m-high mountain by cable car (page 39)

2 Cape of Good Hope
Wonderful views out over the sea and the Cape Peninsula (page 43)

3 Plettenberg Bay
The most beautiful seaside resort on the Garden Route (page 56)

4 Stellenbosch
The second oldest town in South Africa is at the very centre of the wine-growing area (page 61)

5 Kirstenbosch Botanical Gardens
The best time to visit the botanical gardens on the slopes of Table Mountain in Cape Town is in spring, i.e. from August to October (page 39)

6 Kalahari Gemsbok Park
It is claimed to be the most beautiful wildlife park in southern Africa (page 54)

7 Cango Caves
These limestone caves near Oudtshoorn are among the most interesting caverns in the world (page 50)

Namaqualand in the spring: a riot of colour across the bare landscape

Mossel Bay but experienced a rather unfriendly reception from the Hottentots who pelted him and his crew with stones. Ten years later in 1488, they gave Vasco da Gama a much friendlier welcome. He initiated the first trade link with the Hottentots by exchanging jewellery made from glass beads for a bull.

Today Port Elizabeth is an important centre for the automobile production industry. In spite of numerous other industries and a well-developed economic structure, including a modern harbour, the town is still a popular holiday destination. 'PE', as it is often called, is situated on Algoa Bay and has wonderful beaches. The same can be said of East London which was developed by German settlers at the mouth of the Buffalo River. It is the only town in South Africa with a river port.

The attraction of the Cape Provinces is due not least to its rich and varied landscapes. The West Coast, for example, is much more arid than the 'gardens' of the East Coast. Arriving at the Langebaan Lagoon and seeing all the Churchhaven fisher cottages is like stumbling across an idyllic Greek village. Further inland is

Namaqualand which presents a fairly barren view for most of the year until, in October after the rains, the landscape is transformed and covered with a carpet of flowers. Wild flowers in a variety of colours stretch for kilometres. This view is best enjoyed from the Vanrhyns Pass. Beyond this to the north there is the fascinating Kalahari Desert with its game park and the famous Augrabies Falls.

CAPE TOWN

(**116/A–B5**) Many visitors, even the well-travelled, claim that Cape Town is the most beautiful city in the world. The people who live here are certainly convinced of this fact. The best view of the harbour is seen by those who arrive by sea. The sight of the Table Mountain with the town on its slopes is stunning. In the summer it is often shrouded in a 'tablecloth' of cloud which descends on the large flat mountain and then evaporates in the warm air. Just as beautiful is the view from Robben Island, a former prison most of which is a nature reserve. Visitors can go and see the cell where Nelson Mandela was formerly imprisoned. On the city side of Table Mountain is the harbour. It was built right out into the sea to ensure that it was deep enough, since the seabed was extremely rocky. Piers were constructed into the sea and the seabed was built up with earth. The reclaimed land is called the *Foreshore.* The oldest part of the harbour is the Victoria and Alfred Dock which is now a popular area for recreation, full of shops and restaurants.

Cape Town is the 'mother town' of South Africa, the oldest town in the country. When Jan van Riebeeck arrived here with his little fleet of three ships and 125 pioneers (including four women), the Dutch East India Company had no intention of establishing a town. All that was planned was a supply port for ships on their way east. 27 years after Riebeeck's arrival there were only 700 people living in the settlement. When Simon van der Stel was appointed commandant, immigrants were also allowed to settle on the Cape. During his twenty years in office, van der Stel transformed the isolated trading post into a flourishing colony.

Today Cape Town has a population of over four million. It is the second largest city after Johannesburg. The city mainly supports itself through the harbour and through tourism. It is also South Africa's parliamentary capital. With the 1910 Union of South Africa, it was decided that Pretoria should be the seat of government but that the Parliament should be resident in Cape Town for six months of each year starting February. Thus, during the most beautiful season of the year, the ministers, secretaries and assistants move with their families to the seaside. All the embassies and their staff come too.

The Capetonians are cheerful people who know how to enjoy themselves. Spoilt by the beauty of the area and the fact that there are so many exciting things going on, they lead a comparatively stress-free existence. There is time for everything and everything takes time. Visitors from other parts of the country call this attitude the 'Cape coma'.

Business people from Johannesburg for whom time is money often feel close to despair here. For someone who is used to racing along the city highways of Johannesburg, it is incomprehensible that no-one in Cape Town is in the least perturbed to have to wait a few minutes in the crowded city centre, as someone makes an awkward attempt at parking.

SIGHTS

☞ City Map inside back cover

Castle of Good Hope (U/C5–6)
This castle was the residence of the first governors of the Cape. It was built in 1666 and is the oldest building in South Africa. It is shaped like a pentagon and was constructed as a fort with cannon emplacements to protect the first settlers. It is now home to an Afrikana collection and there is also the Maritime and Military Museum. *Castle St.; daily 10 am–4 pm; guided tours daily at 10 and 11 am, 12, 2 and 3 pm; Dec–Jan every 30 minutes.*

Company's Garden (U/A4)

Near the Groote Kerk is the beginning of Government Avenue, a pedestrian street lined with oaks which is almost one kilometre long. It connects the city centre with the suburbs at the foot of Table Mountain. On the right hand side is Company's Garden. It was laid out in 1652 by Jan van Riebeeck so that the ships could be supplied with fresh vegetables.

The Groot Constantia wine estate

Groot Constantia (O)

This historic wine estate is a perfect example of Cape Dutch architecture. It now houses a museum of 17th century furniture as well as a collection of paintings and porcelain. In the old wine cellar there is also a wine museum. Constantia wines have a long history and were drunk in the courts of Europe at the time of Napoleon. *There is a restaurant and wine tasting takes place daily 9 am–4.30 pm; Tel. 021/794-51 28; Groot Constantia Rd.; museum daily 10 am–5 pm*

Bo-Kaap (U/B3)

Many descendants of the Malayan slaves live here in small colourful houses. The *Bo-Kaap Museum* in *Wale St.* illustrates what life was like in a Muslim family in the last century. *Tanabaru Tours* offers tours by well-informed guides and will organise dinner with a local family. *Tel. 021/24 07 19*

Parliament and Tuynhuis (U/A–B4)

On the left side of Government Avenue, the rear of the Parliament is visible. During the months when the Parliament is sitting it can be visited by prior arrangement. Next to it is the Tuynhuis, the official residence

of the President, built in 1751 and set in a botanical garden. *Guided tours Mon–Fri 11 am and 2 pm; Tel. 021/403-24 60; Government Ave.*

St. George's Cathedral (U/B4)

The cathedral of the Anglican archbishop of South Africa. It was built by the well-known British architect, Sir Herbert Baker, who spent a number of years living in South Africa. *Wale St.*

Table Mountain and Kirstenbosch Botanical Gardens (O)

★ ↘ The cable car takes five minutes to reach the summit of Table Mountain, 1,086 m above the city. The view is breathtaking. Almost all of the Cape Peninsula is visible from this vantage point. The cable car operates all year round, weather permitting. This basically means providing that it is not windy in Cape Town. *From Dec to Apr the cable car operates daily from 8.30 am to 10 pm and from May to Nov daily from 8.30 am to 5 pm. Round trip costs around 34 R.*

Right on Table Mountain, at a height of 100 to 1,000 m, there is a National Park, the ★ *Kirstenbosch Botanical Gardens.*

Nearly all of the 22,000 plants which grow in South Africa can be found here over an area of 560 hectares. An enormous glass house known as the 'Glass Cathedral' houses a restaurant as well as exhibitions. The best time to visit is from August to October. *Sep–March daily 6 am–7 pm, Apr–Aug daily 6 am–6 pm; admission approx. 4 R.*

Victoria & Alfred Waterfront (U/E1–2)

⊙ ⚹ Named after the British Queen Victoria and her second son, Alfred, who laid the foundation for the new harbour basin in 1860, there are restaurants here to suit every taste. In addition there are museums, hotels, theatres and cinemas. Every good shop in Cape Town has a branch in the two shopping centres. Watching the sunset while enjoying a glass of wine on the quay or on a sunset cruise in a sail boat is an experience not to be missed. The sensational *Two Oceans Aquarium (daily 10 am–6.30 pm; admission approx. 18 R)* is definitely worth a visit, offering a chance to see the marine inhabitants of both oceans. *Waterfront Visitors Centre; Tel. 021/418-23 69; Fax 25 21 65; e-mail: info@waterfront.co.za*

MUSEUMS

District Six Museum (U/B5)

Photographic exhibition of the violent expulsion of all the inhabitants of this area by the apartheid government. *25 a Buitenkant St.; Mon–Sat 10 am–4.30 pm*

Robben Island Museum (O)

Those who wish to visit the prison island where Mandela

and other political prisoners were kept should be sure to book a place on the ferry well in advance. *Clocktower Terminal, Waterfront; Tel. 021/419-13 00; admission approx. 52 R per person*

South African Museum (U/A4)

The natural history museum is situated at one end of the Botanical Gardens. The section on the life of the Bushmen is particularly interesting. *Queen Victoria St.; daily 10 am–5 pm*

RESTAURANTS

Marco's Africa Place (U/C3)

The best dishes from the cooking pots of Africa. *15 Rose Lane, Bo-Kaap; Tel. 021/423-54 12; category 3*

Alphen (O)

The restaurant in the manor house serves top European dishes with an African flair. *Alphen Dr., Constantia; Tel. 021/794-50 11; category 2*

Blue Danube (O)

⧫ Not only does Thomas Sinn serve the best food in Cape Town, the restaurant also boasts a beautiful view of Table Mountain. *102 New Church St., Tamberskloof; Tel. 021/423-36 24; category 1*

Café Paradiso (U/A4)

⚹ Particularly recommended for breakfast and lunch. *110 Kloof St., Gardens; Tel. 021/423-86 53; category 2*

Noon Gun (U/B3)

⧫ Malayan restaurant above the Bo-Kaap. Has a beautiful view over the city. No alcohol. *273 Longmarket St., Signal Hill; Tel. 021/424-05 29; category 3*

San Marco (O)

❖ Luigi Scaglia has been delighting diners for years with the best Italian food to be found in the city. *92 Main Rd., Sea Point; Tel. 021/439-27 58; category 2*

Vilamoura (O)

⟋ Wonderful fish dishes, prepared in Mozambique style. The restaurant is situated on the beach in Camps Bay. *Victoria Rd., Camps Bay; Tel. 021/438-18 50; category 1*

African Craft Market (O)

In Khayelisha Township. Authentic handicrafts by black South Africans. The minibus owner, Peter, brings a group here every Monday and Thursday. *Tel. 083/310-64 54*

Art Safari (U/B3)

Not only does the Lipschitz Gallery have works by local artists, customers are also taken to their studios. *138 Buitengracht, Bo-Kaap; Tel. 021/422-02 80*

Bygone Antiques (O)

Antiques, South African linen and silver are on sale in an old wine cellar which is situated in a beautiful award-winning garden. *8 Augusta's Way, Constantia; Tel. 021/794-54 89*

HOTELS

Cape Heritage Hotel (U/C3)

The rooms of this excellent hotel in the city centre are situated in a number of houses arranged around a courtyard. *17 rms; 90 Bree St.; Tel. 021/424-46 46; Fax 424-49 49; e-mail: chrelais@satis. co.za; category 2*

ikhaya (U/A5)

𝝒 The name means 'home' in Xhosa. Guests certainly feel at home in the rooms which are decorated in African style. *16 rms; Wandel St., Gardens; Tel. 021/461-88 80; Fax 461-88 89; e-mail: ikhaya@iaafrica.com; category 3*

Villa Via (O)

⟋ The hotel is situated right on the shore of the Ocean. *201 rms; Beach Rd., Granger Bay; Tel. 021/418-57 29; Fax 418-57 17; e-mail: vvgb@iaafrica.com; category 2*

Mount Nelson (O)

This is a luxury colonial hotel which was built in 1899. It is situated in the middle of a large park not far from the city centre. When Winston Churchill was working as a war correspondent during the Boer War, he drank tea on the terrace here. *159 rms; Orange St.; Tel. 021/423-10 00; Fax 24 74 72; category 1*

In the spirit of Marco Polo

Marco Polo was the first true world traveller. He travelled with peaceful intentions forging links between the East and the West. His aim was to discover the world, and explore different cultures and environments without changing or disrupting them. He is an excellent role model for the travellers of today and the future. Wherever we travel we should show respect for other peoples and the natural world.

WWF

Sailing boats and deep sea yachts can be hired at the harbour, *Bookings at Tel. 021/ 448-44 41.* Deep sea fishing is also available *(Tel. 021/439-82 70).* Surfing and windsurfing can be enjoyed on many beaches *(Tel. 021/64 29 72).* Visitors who wish to play golf in Cape Town should contact *Royal Cape Golf Club; Tel. 021/761-65 51.*

Clifton (O)
❂ The four Clifton beaches are the most beautiful in Cape Town. Always sheltered from the wind, they are perfect for sunbathing and surfing. However, the Atlantic Ocean is never warmer than 17°C (63°F), even in summer.

ENTERTAINMENT

⚘❂ The places with most happenings are the *Waterfront* pubs in the harbour or in *Long Street* and *Kloof Street.* Also recommended:

Baraza (O)
⚘ Bar with a sea view. *Victoria Rd., Camps Bay; Tel. 021/438-17 58*

Mano's (O)
Bar and restaurant with a great atmosphere. *39 Main Rd., Green Point; Tel. 021/434-10 90*

From the top of ꙮ Signal Hill the view over Cape Town at night is fantastic.

INFORMATION

Western Cape Tourism (U/C4)
Pinnacle Building; Corner of Burg Street and Castle Street; Tel. 021/426-56 39; Fax 426-56 40; e-mail: wetbcape@iafrica.com

SURROUNDING AREA

Bloubergstrand (116/B5)
ꙮ In 1806, this was the site of the battle between the British and the Boers which led to the eventual occupation of the Cape. There is a magnificent view of Table Mountain and Cape Town. The place got its name because Table Mountain often appears shrouded in a blue haze from here. The beach is perfect for windsurfing and angling. If you wish to dine here, a good place to go is: *Ons Huisie, Stadler Rd.; Tel. 021/56 15 53; category 2*

The view of Table Mountain from Bloubergstrand is stunning

Cape of Good Hope   (116/B6)

★ ↘↙ The Cape of Good Hope lies at the southern tip of the Cape Peninsula, surrounded by a nature reserve. Incidentally, contrary to popular opinion, it is not the southernmost tip of Africa. When Bartholomeu Dias sailed round the Cape for the first time, he called it the Cape of Storms. Since it is often very windy here, it is important to check the weather forecast before embarking on an excursion. From the parking lot a cable car takes visitors to within 40 m of *Cape Point* but for the last few metres, 133 steps must be negotiated on foot. Once at the top, there is a breathtaking view over the sea, with *False Bay* and the Cape Peninsula. The old lighthouse on Cape Point, built in 1836, has long ceased to be operational. The many beaches of the nature reserve are ideal for picnics.

400 m away from the entrance to the nature reserve, there is a very interesting ostrich farm. *Plateau Rd.; Tel. 021/ 78 09 24*

Chapman's Peak Drive   (116/A5–B6)

↘↙ The route from Hout Bay to the Cape of Good Hope takes you along this coastal road which is one of the most beautiful in the world. It was constructed at the beginning of the 1920s by digging into the cliff. 10 km long with steep cliffs above and the roaring ocean below, the view is absolutely spectacular. There is a place in Nordhoek, a small town below the mountain top of Chapman's Peak, where horses are for hire.

Simonstown   (116/B5)

The town was previously the largest British naval base in the southern hemisphere. Its appearance is still very reminiscent of a British harbour town, although Simonstown is now home to the headquarters of the South African navy. The main street is the most historical part of the town: 21 of the houses are over 150 years old.

CALEDON

(116/C5) The Caledon Springs, six warm ones and one cold, attracted visitors from Europe as long ago as the turn of the century. The town is one of the oldest in the country and is situated at the foot of Swartberg. There are extensive opportunities for walking in the area around Caledon.

SIGHTS

Victoria Wild Flower and Garden Reserve

Anyone who wants to visit this wild flower garden should allow half a day for it. The floral splendour which covers an area of ten hectares is incredible. *Mon–Sat 8.30 am–5 pm*

MUSEUM

Caledon Museum

The museum portrays how South Africans used to live in Victorian times. One of the nine cannons with which the farmers of the area formerly had to defend themselves now stands in front of the museum. *11 Constitution St.; Mon–Fri 8 am–5 pm; Sat 9 am–12 pm*

Libanon B&B

Romantic rooms in a house built in the Cape Dutch style. *4 rms; 21 Krige St.; Tel. 028/214-10 96; category 3*

Tourism Bureau

22 Plein St.; Mon–Fri 8 am–1 pm and 2 pm–4.30 pm, Sat 9 am–1 pm; Tel. 028/212-15 11

Cape Agulhas (116/C6)

Cape Agulhas is the southernmost point of Africa, although this tip is much less spectacular than the Cape of Good Hope. The name Agulhas is Portuguese and means needles, which refers to the dozens of sharp little rocks and reefs which are extremely dangerous for ships. The lighthouse was built in 1848 and it is open to visitors every day between 11 am and 3 pm. At night the lighthouse beams out its warning to ships with a light which has a brightness equivalent to 11 million candles.

Greyton (116/C5)

This town, only 46 km from Caledon, boasts excellent and attractive places to stay, e.g. the *Greyton Lodge; 18 rms; 46 Main Rd.; Tel. 028/254-98 76; Fax 254-96 72; category 2.* Don't miss the original delicatessen *The Oak and Vigne, Ds. Botha St.; Tel. 028/254-90 37.*

Hermanus (116/B6)

❖ ✗ One of the most popular holiday resorts in South Africa. It

Cape Agulhas, the southernmost tip of the continent

is often the destination of Capetonians for a weekend excursion. It is especially busy during the summer months. Hermanus is beautifully situated with romantic beaches. The lagoon called *De Mond* at the mouth of the little river is a paradise for water sports enthusiasts. It is also deemed by anglers to be one of the best fishing grounds. In addition, between July and November, the whales gather here to mate and give birth to their young. Right on the shore of the ocean are the *Windsor Hotel, 60 rms; Marine Drive, Tel. 028/312-37 27; Fax 312-21 81; e-mail: info@windsorhotel.com; category 2,* and the best restaurant in town, *The Burgundy; Market Square; Tel. 028/312-28 00; category 2*

Sir Lowry's Pass (116/B5)

〰 The Pass affords a fantastic panorama. Right on the road is the Howhoek Inn, the oldest hotel in South Africa, set in a wonderful garden. This was formerly the place where journeys were broken to change over the horses. *18 rms; Tel. 028/492-96 46; Fax 492-91 12; category 3*

44

EAST LONDON

(119/F4) East London (pop. 200,000) is a popular holiday destination even amongst the locals. This is no surprise, considering that there are wonderful beaches and an average of seven hours of sunshine every day. In early colonial times, the town marked the border between the British and the Xhosa tribes. The series of Frontier Wars between 1779 and 1838 cost many fighters their lives. So despairing were the Xhosa that they turned to the prophecies of a nine-year-old girl. In 1856 Nongquase told them that all the whites would be chased into the sea by the ancestors, provided that the Xhosa sacrificed all their supplies and all their animals. As a result of this 20,000 people starved to death and the 40,000 who survived were forced to leave their land.

Until 1857, when 2,400 German settlers arrived here, East London was principally a military base. The Germans were meant to be fighting for Queen Victoria in the Crimean War but they landed in the British colony of South Africa. Their influence can still be seen today, surviving in a large number of place names, such as Berlin, Hamburg, Braunschweig and many others.

SIGHTS

German Settlers' Memorial
Memorial to the first German settlers. The sculptor, Lipschitz, made the memorial from bronze. It depicts a mother, a father and a child who left their homeland. *Esplanade*

Harbour
Look out for the John Baillie Memorial which commemorates the man who raised the first British flag here.

MUSEUM

East London Museum
This natural history museum is world-famous because of the coelacanth, a prehistoric fish with four limb-like fins. Before it was caught in 1938, it was thought that this species had become extinct 60 million years ago. In addition, the museum boasts a dodo egg which was brought from Mauritius. It is believed to be the only specimen in the world, as the dodo long ago became extinct. The anthropological section illustrates the tribal traditions of the Xhosa peoples from the nearby areas of Transkei and Ciskei. *319 Oxford St.; Mon–Fri 9.30 am–5 pm, Sat 9.30 am–12 pm*

RESTAURANTS

Bellami's
Here meals are prepared for the diners by the whole family. *18 Marine Terrace, Beach Front; 0431/43 21 45; category 2*

Crawford's Cabins
Above a beach, just out of town. The menu ranges from Eisbein (a German dish of boiled pork served with sauerkraut) to Xhosa dishes. *Cintsa East; Tel. 0431/38 50 00; category 2*

SHOPPING

Lock Street Gaol
The former cells of this prison which was built in 1880, now house a number of shops, selling

handicrafts and souvenirs. Visitors can also have a look at the death cells, some of which have been preserved, and the gallows. The last execution took place here in 1935. *Lock St.*

HOTEL

Kennaway
Situated right on the shore. *88 rms; Beach Front; Tel. 0431/255 31; Fax 213 26; category 2*

SPORTS & LEISURE

Diving
Diving here can become a bit of a treasure hunt. There are a number of wrecks within a fairly small area. On 26 May 1872 alone seven ships sank near East London. *Information Tel. 083/275-80 07*

Windsurfing, sailing
There are excellent opportunities for windsurfing, sailing and canoeing at the Bridal Drift Dam. Overnight accommodation in huts. *Tel. 0431/46 27 77*

INFORMATION

Tourism Bureau
Old Library Building, Argyle St.; Mon–Fri 8.30 am–4.30 pm, Sat 8.30 am–11 am; Tel. 0431/260 15

SURROUNDING AREA

King William's Town   (119/F4)
This town was originally a missionary station. In 1835 it was destroyed by Xhosa tribes. After the British had established a military base here, the missionaries returned and founded the town. In 1858, 2,000 German settlers arrived here, in the hope of finding a better life. However, many of them starved to death. Today the *Kaffrarian Museum (Alexander Rd.; Mon–Fri 9 am–12.45 pm and 2 pm–5 pm)* portrays the historical development of the area. King William's Town is also the birthplace of Steve Biko, the freedom fighter who was murdered by the police in 1977. His grave can be seen in a cemetery in *Cathcart St.,* just outside the town towards Grahamstown.

Wild Coast   (114/C6–115/E4)
The Wild Coast is the coast of the Transkei. The beaches extend for over 250 km. The area is not, in fact, especially wild and it has some of the most beautiful beaches in South Africa. Between the green hills, on the shores of lagoons and the banks of rivers, the white round huts of the Xhosa can be seen. One of the larger places here is Port

---

Show Houses

A popular Sunday activity amongst South Africans is to visit a 'show house'. The owners, who wish to sell their houses, allow estate agents to show potential buyers their houses on Sunday afternoons. However, lots of other people who have no intention of moving, attracted by large signs in front of the houses or by lavish adverts, also come along out of curiosity. There's nothing more interesting than seeing how other people live.

St. Johns, a little harbour town at the mouth of the Umzimvubu River. The rocks and cliffs are ideal for walking and women sell fish and oysters very cheaply here.

On the Wild Coast there is also the *Wild Coast Sun Hotel*, one of the most attractive of this chain in South Africa. It serves excellent food and also offers casinos and a golf course which is right on the shore. *Situated between the mouths of the Umtavuna and Mzamba Rivers; 399 rms; Tel. 039/305-9111; Fax 305-2778; e-mail: wcshotel@suint.co.za; category 1*

FRANSCHHOEK

(**116/B5**) This little wine town is situated in a beautiful valley. It was founded in 1688 by a group of 146 Huguenots who had been forced to leave France where they were persecuted for religious reasons. They named their new home *Le Quartier Français* — the French Quarter. Many of them had come from French wine-growing areas and, because the climate was so similar, they decided to try cultivating vines

here too. The owners of the wine estates in and around Franschhoek have now joined together to become the *Vignerons de Franschhoek*. Wine tasting is offered at almost all of the estates. *Information Tel. 021/876-3062*

SIGHTS

Franschhoek Pass
❧ Surely the most beautiful mountain pass in the area. It affords wonderful views across the valley. The first settlers called it the Elephant Pass because elephants and herds of other animals crossed the mountain on this path.

SHOPPING

La Grange de Cabriere
A large selection of African art in a stylish atmosphere. *Cabriere Rd.; Tel. 021/876-2155*

MUSEUM

Huguenot Memorial Museum
The museum depicts the history of the Huguenots and the first settlers. *Lambrecht St.; Mon–Sat 8 am–5 pm, Sun 2 pm–5 pm*

RESTAURANTS

Chez Michel
This little restaurant is centrally located in the main street. Peter and Bradley, the owners, take care of their guests, personally. *Main Rd.; Tel. 021/876-2671; category 2*

La Petite Ferme
❧ This tourist café is situated at the Franschhoek Pass. The salmon trout is particularly recom-

Huguenot Museum, Franschhoek

mended. *Pass Rd.; Tel. 021/876 30 16; category 3*

The Riverside

Unusual restaurant with a garden on the banks of the Berg River. The dishes served here are works of art. On the R 45 near the Berg River Bridge. *Tel. 021/874 20 58; category 2*

ACCOMMODATION

Auberge du Quartier Français

A country hotel which achieves the perfect combination of European chic and South African hospitality. *16 rms; Berg St.; Tel. 021/876 21 51; Fax 876-36 30; category 1*

Klein Dassenberg

↘↗ Self-catering holiday cottages with a wonderful view. On the R 45, last road on the right before the town. *Tel. + Fax 021/876-21 07; category 3*

La Provence Farms

The once-enormous wine farm, La Provence, has now been divided up. Overnight accommodation is offered by three wine estates. *Grande Provence; 5 rms; Tel. 021/876-21 63; Fax 876-42 04; e-mail: orders@ agustawines.co.za; category 2; Basse Provence; 4 rms; Tel. 021/876-29 94; Fax 876-29 95; e-mail: booking@ basse.provence.co.za; category 2; La Provence; 4 rms; Tel. 021/876-21 63.* All the farms are situated on the R 45 towards Franschhoek.

INFORMATION

Franschhoek Tourist Information

Huguenot Rd.; Mon–Fri 9 am–5 pm, Sat 9 am–1 pm; Tel. 021/876 36 30

SURROUNDING AREA

Boschendal   (116/B5)

This wine estate is one of the most magnificent in South Africa. It is situated in the lovely landscape of the Drakensteintal Valley. The estate was established by a Huguenot family, the de Villiers, who lived here for 200 years until the end of the last century. It now belongs to the mineral company, Anglo-American. The manor house is a *Museum*, decorated in the style of a traditional Cape family house. *(daily 11 am–4 pm).*

Nearby there is *a restaurant and a wine bar,* where visitors can try the Boschendal wines which are famous far beyond the borders of South Africa. *Tel. 021/874 - 12 52.* In the summer the old trees on the estate invite visitors to sit and enjoy a picnic. *Category 3; wine tasting Mon–Fri 8.30 am–5 pm, Sat 8.30 am–12.30 pm*

Tulbagh   (116/B4)

This small historical town is situated in the middle of a fruit-growing area. It is well-known for the many houses built in the Cape Dutch style. All the buildings in *Church St.* are classified as historic monuments. In 1969 there was an earthquake which almost completely destroyed Tulbagh. With great care and at considerable expense the inhabitants rebuilt and restored the town. The *Oude Kerk*, the old church, houses a selection of chairs collected over the centuries. They are the former church chairs and some of them still display the names of the people for whom they were reserved.

♣ One of the best restaurants on

the Cape is the *Paddagang* in Tulbagh. The name means 'frog crossing' and its derivation is disputed. Diners can sit in the garden under the trees and vine leaves, surrounded by roses, and try the dishes of the Cape area. *Church St.; Tel. 023/230-02 42; category 3*

It is well worth spending a night at *Rijk's Ridge Country House.* 2 km outside Tulbaghs. *Tel. 023/230-1006; Fax 230-1125; e-mail: neville @ rijksridge. co. za; category 2*

GEORGE

(117/F5) The largest town on the Garden Route is situated at the feet of the Outeniqua Mountains. It is surrounded by an incredibly beautiful, park-like landscape right on the shore. Visitors approaching George from inland come through the Montagu or Outeniqua Pass, built by Italian prisoners of war during World War II. Walking through the town, it is well worth stopping at the book shop in York Street. One of the old oaks in front of the building is protected by a preservation order. The *Old Slave Tree* is where the slaves used to be sold. The pretty *St. Mark's Cathedral* is also noteworthy. It is supposed to be the smallest cathedral on the continent.

SIGHTS

Outeniqua Choo Tjoe

The old steam locomotive takes visitors on a wonderful route through tunnels, across lagoons, beside lakes and along the coast to Knysna. The day trip can only be made on week days, except during school holidays, when the train also runs on Saturdays. One trip takes three hours. *Tickets from the station*

MUSEUM

George Museum

This museum is in an old court building. Visitors can learn all about different types of wood and how it is worked. Original pieces of furniture which are made from the African woods *Yellowwood* and *Stinkwood* are crafted in this area. There is also a collection of antique musical instruments. *Old Drostdy Building, Courtenay St.; Mon–Fri 9 am–4.30 pm, Sat 9 am–12.30 pm*

RESTAURANTS

Copper Pot

❖ Particularly popular with the locals. *12 Montagu St.; Tel. 044/870-7378; category 2*

Red Rock Restaurant

The owner is not only an excellent cook but also paints all the pictures hanging on the walls herself. *Arbour Rd., Glenbarrie; Tel. 044/873-3842; category 3*

HOTEL

Fancourt

A wonderful country house which was built in 1860. The hotel is surrounded by a golf course which produced the legendary South African golf pro, Gary Player. The 27-hole course is available for the use of the guests. *86 rms; Montagu St.; Tel. 044/804-00 00; Fax 804-07 10; e-mail: hotel@fancourt.co.za; category 1*

George is not only popular with visitors because of its beautiful beaches on the Indian Ocean but also for the opportunities it offers for walking. Victoria Bay is known by surfers all over the world.

INFORMATION

Tourist Information Bureau
124 York St.; Mon–Fri 8 am–5.30 pm, Sat 9 am–12 pm; Tel. 044/801- 92 95

SURROUNDING AREA

Cango Caves (117/E4)
★ The huge underground caverns are some of the most fascinating limestone caves in the world. They are 25 million years old. Visitors can observe the unique interaction of colours and shapes. Three guided tours set off, every hour on the hour, between 9 am and 4 pm. They last for thirty, sixty or ninety minutes. *Admission approx. 6–12R; Tel. 044/272- 74 10*

Mossel Bay (117/F5)
A few years ago, after a search which lasted twenty years, oil was found off the coast of this popular harbour and holiday resort. In the 16th century South Africa's very first post office was established in Mossel Bay when a sailor hung a report of his journey in a boot from a milkwood tree. His 'letter' was later found by other sailors. The letters which are posted into the boot-shaped boxes here are still given their own postmarks today. Next to the post-office tree, visitors can still see the spring which was used by Dias to replenish his water supplies. For those who are interested in sea-faring, the *Bartholomeu Dias Museum* is certainly worth a visit. *Mon–Fri 9 am–12.30 pm and 2 pm–3.45 pm.* The town derives its name from the mussels which were highly regarded by sailors as long as 400 years ago. Beyond Mossel Bay there is a highly-recommended country hotel, *Eight Bells on the Mountain Inn,* on the R 328 between Mossel Bay and Oudtshoorn*; 24 rms; Tel. 044/631-00 00; Fax 6 31- 00 04; e-mail: 8bells@mb. lia.net; category 2*

Oudtshoorn (117/F4)
Oudtshoorn is traditionally the world centre for ostrich farming. The locals claim that there is nowhere else in the world where the birds are as successfully reared as they are here. Even before World War I, farmers here earned a fortune with ostrich feathers which were an essential part of fashion at that time. Demand is still high today. Every nine months the birds moult, each one producing one kilogram of feathers. Apart from the feathers, ostrich leather also enjoys great popularity and is made into shoes, handbags, belts and many other items. Legend has it that the oldest ostrich in Oudtshoorn reached the grand old age of 81. There are two farms in the area which offer guided tours. *Highgate; Tel. 044/272-71 15,*and *Safari; Tel. 044/272- 73 11. Both farms are open daily from 7.30 am until 5 pm.* Visitors can also try ostrich steak or an omelette made from an ostrich egg. The *C.P.Nel Museum* illustrates the history of ostrich

Oudtshoorn is the world centre for ostrich farming

rearing. *Baron von Rheede St.; Mon–Sat 9 am–5 pm*

GRAAFF-REINET

(**118/B3**) There are only two towns in the world which are situated in a nature reserve. One of these is Graaff-Reinet. Surrounded by the *Karoo Nature Reserve,* the town is often called 'the gem of the Karoo'. Graaff-Reinet is one of the oldest towns in South Africa. It was founded in 1786 and was named after the Governor, Cornelis Jacob van der Graaff, and his wife, Cornelia Reinet. The heart of the town is rather like a large open-air museum, reflecting the architecture of the last 200 years. Architectural styles range from the low buildings of the Karoo huts to the Cape Dutch estates with their impressive gables and the houses of the Victorian Age. Considerable trouble has been taken to restore all the buildings. There are over 300 houses which are older than any of the buildings in Johannesburg.

MUSEUM

Reinet House and Museum

Visitors who come here can admire a large collection of Cape Dutch furniture as well as an interesting vehicle collection. *Murray St.; Mon–Fri 9 am–12 pm and 3 pm–5 pm; Sat and Sun 10 am–12 pm*

HOTEL

Drostdy Hotel

The hotel is in one of the oldest and certainly most beautiful houses in Graaff-Reinet. The famous architect, Thibauld, whose work is encountered in many places on a trip through the Cape Provinces, designed the building to be the seat of the National Assembly. The building was neglected for decades and had decayed considerably when restoration work began in the 1970s. Now the house once more appears as it would have done in 1806. Guests feel as though they have travelled back in time, especially at dinner which is

Huberta

In the Kaffrarian Museum in King William's Town there is a stuffed hippopotamus. Nothing special, you might think. However, from 1928 to 1931, Hubert (as he was christened) kept the whole nation in suspense. He first appeared in Zululand from where he embarked on a journey which took him hundreds of kilometres across the country. Hubert essentially travelled southwards but with lots of changes of direction and he kept appearing at the oddest moments and in the most improbable places – one morning he was spotted standing in the middle of Durban. He died a violent death, being shot inadvertently by a farmer. Hubert was posthumously renamed Huberta when it was discovered that the animal in question was in fact a female hippopotamus.

served in the former courtroom by candlelight. *51 rms; 28 Church St.; Tel. 0491/221-61; Fax 245-82; category 2*

ENTERTAINMENT

✷ In the evening, the farmers of the area gather in the two bars of the hotel. On Wednesdays, there is always a special event organised, for example, Can-Can dancing on the bar.

INFORMATION

Tourist Information Bureau
Church St.; Mon–Fri 9 am–12.30 pm and 2 pm–5 pm, Sat 9 am–12 pm; Tel. 0491/224-79

SURROUNDING AREA

Karoo Nature Reserve　(117/F3)
This 27,000 hectare park is mainly inhabited by springbok, although there is other game, too. In the middle of the park is the ◁◊▷ *Valley of Desolation,* an interesting geological phenomenon. It is more a ravine than a valley. The erosion of the gorge happened over 200 million years ago

and time seems to have stood still here for an eternity. There are marvellous views over the surrounding area from here. Collecting fossils is prohibited and anyone who ignores this will incur a large fine.

KIMBERLEY

(113/D–E2) When a child found a glittering stone on the banks of the Orange River in 1866, no-one could have imagined that it would lead to the largest diamond rush of all times and that South Africa's diamond town would be established here. The first diamond, named Eureka, weighed 21.25 carat. It can be seen today in the Mine Museum. At first the locals feverishly combed the banks of the river and gradually more and more adventurers from all over the world arrived. The search for the precious stones was successful not only along the river but also under the ground. To start with, Kimberley was little more than a campsite for the tens of thousands of diamond diggers who gave the place the name *New*

Rush. At this time, around 1870, 30,000 people were digging in the so-called *Big Hole,* the largest crater in the world made by humans. It measures about 4.6 km round the circumference and has a diameter of 1.5 km. In 43 years, a total of three tonnes of diamonds was found in this enormous hole. The camp developed into a small town which was given the name Kimberley in 1873.

At around the same time, diamonds were found on *De Beers Farm.* This name is still inextricably linked with diamonds. The global diamond company, De Beers, which is now based in Johannesburg, traces its origins back to Kimberley. All sorts of enigmatic characters came to make their fortunes. One of these was the son of a British parish priest, named Cecil Rhodes. Then there was Barney Barnato, an actor and boxer, also from Britain. They made Kimberley into a highly-developed town, with the first street lighting in South Africa, a tramway, the first stock exchange and an aviation school.

SIGHTS

Big Hole and Kimberley Museum

Near the crater, parts of the town have been reconstructed to the way they were at the time of the diamond rush.There are a number of observation spots to view the large hole. The diamond pavilion houses probably the largest collection of uncut diamonds in the world. One of these stones is the world's largest uncut diamond, weighing 616 carats; it is simply called '616'. *Bulfontein St.; daily 8 am–6 pm*

Bulfontein Diamond Recovery Plant

A modern diamond mine. *Molyneux Rd.; Tel. 0531/82 96 51; guided tours Mon, Wed–Fri 8 am, Tues 9.30 am*

Steam Locomotive Shunting Yards

Visitors can see forty of Kimberley's old steam locomotives in the old shunting yards and at Witput Station. *Oliver St.; southbound. Information Tel. 0531/88 22 25.* Phone in advance.

Tram Service

The tram (1913) operates several times a day between the Market Square and the Big Hole. *Tickets can be bought on board; daily 9 am–4 pm*

MUSEUM

McGregor Museum

The house was built by Rhodes as a sanatorium. Now it is a museum which portrays how the diamond kings lived in Kimberley at the end of the last century. *Egerton Rd.; Mon–Sat 9 am– 5 pm, Sun 2 pm–5 pm*

RESTAURANTS

Halfway House Pub

✪ The pub was opened in 1880. At that time the diners arrived on horseback. The sign above the entrance shows Cecil Rhodes arriving. *229 Du Toitspan Rd.; Tel. 0531/82 51 51; category 3*

Star of the West Pub

This pub is one of the oldest in South Africa. The barstool which was made specially for Cecil Rhodes can still be seen. *West Circular Rd.; Tel. 0531/822-64 63; category 3*

Edgerton House

The guest house is located directly opposite the McGregor Museum. It is protected by a preservation order. *13 rms; 5 Egerton Rd.; Tel. 0531/81 18 71; Fax 81 17 85; category 3*

Savoy Hotel

Magnificent hotel with the charm of the Old World and the comfort of the New. *42 rms; De Beers Rd.; Tel. 0531/82 62 11; Fax 82 70 21; category 2*

INFORMATION

Tourist Information Office

City Civic Complex, Bulfontein Rd.; Mon–Fri 9 am–3 pm, Sat 8.30 am–11.30 am; Tel. 0531/82 72 98

SURROUNDING AREA

Augrabies Falls (111/E2)

The name of the falls comes from the language of the Hottentots. It means 'Place of great noise' which relates to the first cascade, where the Orange River plunges 56 m into a deep, narrow gorge. The pool beneath is 130 m deep and legend has it that there are diamonds worth a fortune at the bottom which have been swept there by the river. However, the force of the water thundering down makes any diving exploration pointless.

Barkly West (113/D2)

This was where the hunt for diamonds began and diggers can still be seen occasionally today. Anyone who wishes to try their luck can get a permit from the local police between June and September. On Saturdays the diggers bring the diamonds they have found into town and sell them. There is also an open-air archaeological museum here which shows all the things which have been found during the hunt for diamonds. *Daily 9 am–4 pm*

Kalahari Gemsbok Park (104/A–C1–B3)

★ The park is the largest untouched ecosystem in the world. Together with the Botswana National Park it covers an area of over two million hectares. It is home to many animals, including lions, cheetahs, foxes, gemsbok, springbok and antelope. The park is open to visitors all year round but the best time to go is the period from March to May or in September and October. Overnight accommodation is available in huts at three camps. *On the B 3, through Upingtonin the direction of Botswana; Tel. 012/343-19 91*

KNYSNA

(118/A5) This charming and colourful town is one of the very popular destinations on the Garden Route. Knysna is beautifully situated in the mountains, with huge forests, a large lagoon and the sea nearby. The town was founded in 1804 by George Rex. His extravagant lifestyle fuelled the rumours that he was the illegitimate son of the English king George III and that, after his father unexpectedly became king, he was forced to leave Britain. It was one of George Rex's ships which was the first to navigate the channel between the lagoon and the sea. This channel is

Plettenberg Bay: the bay is lined with luxury holiday homes

flanked by two sandstone cliffs called the *Knysna Heads*. Oysters are cultivated in the 13 km² lagoon. They are considered to be among the best in the world.

SIGHTS

King Edward Tree
This enormous yellowwood tree is 600 years old. It has a circumference of 6 m and is 40 m tall. It stands in the Knysna Forest.

Knysna Forest
This forest is the largest in South Africa and extends from George over 170 km eastwards along the Outeniqua and Tsitsikamma Mountains. As well as the many yellowwood trees, valuable stinkwood trees also grow here. Some of them are as much as 800 years old. In some places the forest is as dense as a jungle. The Knysna Forest is not only home to a wide variety of different birds but also to the few Knysna elephants which still remain today.

MUSEUM

Knysna Museum
Exhibition about the history of the town. *Corner of Main St. and Queen St.; Mon–Fri 9 am–4.30 pm, Sat 9.30 am–1 pm*

RESTAURANTS

La Loerie
The name La Loerie is taken from the famous bird which is found in this area. *Main Rd.; Tel. 044/382-16 16; category 2*

Oysters
⚹ This restaurant is an absolute must for people who enjoy fish dishes. *Pledge Sq.; Tel. 044/382-66 41; category 1*

Pink Umbrella
In the past, food was only served in the beautiful garden. Now there is also a small dining room. The restaurant is open at lunchtime all year round but dinner is only served during high season. *14 King's Way; Tel. 044/384-01 35; category 3*

HOTELS

Belvidere Manor
A very good hotel in a historical manor house with a view over the lagoon and the forest. *30 Cottages, Belvidere Estate; Tel. 044/387-10 55; Fax 387-10 59; e-mail: manager@belvidere.co.za; category 2*

Parkes Manor
Country house in victorian style, set in a park with a wonderful view. *9 rms; Azalea St.; Tel. 044/382-51 00; Fax 382-51 24; e-mail: parkes@gardenroute.ca; category 1*

SPORTS & LEISURE

Elephant Walk
A 21-km-long walk through the Knysna Forest. The route begins in Knysna and is signposted well. It takes about six hours. There are also two other shorter routes.

House boats
There are opportunities for water sports of all kinds on the lagoon. House boats can be rented and it is an exciting experience to spend the night on one. *Lightley's in Bluewaters; Tel. 0445/387-10 26; Fax 387-10 67; category 3*

INFORMATION

Tourism Information Bureau
40 Main St.; Mon–Fri 8.30 am–6 pm, Sat 9 am–3 pm, Sun 9 am–1 pm; Tel. 044/382-70 78

SURROUNDING AREA

Plettenberg Bay (118/A5)
★ In 1576 the Portuguese explorer, Mesquita da Perestrelo, gave the place the name *Bahia Formosa,* which means beautiful bay. In 1778, the Governor of the time, Joachim von Plettenberg, came here. He was so impressed with the bay that he gave his own name to the area. Nowadays Plettenberg Bay is an exclusive seaside resort with three wonderful beaches which extend over 11 km. In some places, the calm, warm water is ideal for children. On average the sun shines 320 days each year. Between July and September, whales give birth to their young in the bay.

The former Plettenberg Whaling Station is now a *hotel,* the *Beacon Island.* The architecturally spectacular building is situated on a spit of land, surrounded by the sea where whales and dolphins frolic. *200 rms; Tel. 044/533-11 20; Fax 533-28 80; category 2.*

Above the beach with a wide view across the Indian Ocean is the *Plettenberg.* It is very elegant and is smaller and more intimate than the Beacon Island. *40 rms; Tel. 044/533-20 30; Fax 533-20 74; category 1.*

There are two highly-recommended *restaurants* in 'Plett', as the locals call Plettenberg for short. One is the *Islander,* which is one of the best fish restaurants in South Africa, *Tel. 044/533-77 76; category 2.* The other is *The Boardwalk; Yellowwood Building, Main St.; Tel. 044/533-14 20; category 3.* It serves very good homestyle cooking.

Tsitsikamma Coastal National Park (118/A–B5)
This park extends over 100 km from Plettenberg Bay as far as the mouth of the Groot River. The protected area does not only include the coastal zone but also

takes in a five-kilometre strip of the ocean. Inland from here lies the Tsitsikamma Forest National Park within the boundaries of which a piece of the enormous forest that once covered the area is preserved. The ✺ *Paul Sauer Bridge* is very impressive. It is 192 m long and spans the Storms River at a height of 139 m. The view from here is breathtaking. Visitors looking for overnight accommodation in this lovely green landscape should try the *Old Village Inn; 49 rms; Stormsrivier; Tel. 042/541-17 11; Fax 541-16 69; e-mail: the_inn@global.co.za; category 3*

LANGEBAAN

(116/A4) This little town is situated at the beginning of the Langebaan Lagoon which is 16 km long, 5 km wide and only 6 km deep. It is a paradise for birds and in summer 55,000 of them live here, including flamingos and cormorants. Langebaan is a popular holiday destination for water sports enthusiasts, divers and anglers, not least because of the warm water.

SIGHTS

Churchhaven
A romantic fishing village with old houses on the shores of the lagoon.

HOTEL

Farmhouse Langebaan
Parts of this hotel are in an old farm house which affords very impressive views over the lagoon. Visitors can watch flamingos and dolphins from the ter-

race of the hotel. *15 rms; 5 Egret St.; Tel. 022/772-20 62; Fax 772-19 80; e-mail: farmhous@cis.co.za; category 3*

SURROUNDING AREA

Saldanha   (116/A4)
This town was named after one of the first Portuguese generals. He arrived here by ship in 1503. If he had found water here all those years ago, Saldanha would now be a much more important harbour town than Cape Town. The bay forms one of the largest natural harbours in the world. In addition, it is ideally situated for the export of iron ore. The restaurants in the area around the harbour serve excellent, simple seafood dishes. For example at the *Meresteijn; Main Rd.; Tel. 022/714-33 45; category 2.* Information from the *Westcoast Publicity Ass.; Tel. 022/714-20 88.*

PAARL

(116/B5) Paarl is the largest inland town on the Cape. It was founded in 1717 and takes its name from the massive cliff which, when the sun is in a certain position in the sky, shimmers like a pearl. The town played a significant role in the development of the world's newest language, Afrikaans. It was first officially introduced here in 1875. This is commemorated by the only language monument in the world. As well as for the Afrikaners, Paarl is also a special place for the supporters of the ANC. In 1990, Nelson Mandela was released from the 'Victor Verster' prison here.

A trip on the luxurious Blue Train is an unforgettable experience

SIGHTS

KWV
The wine and brandy cellars here are the largest in the world. Over one hundred fine beverages are produced here. There are guided tours round the cellars. *Kohler St.; Tel. 021/807-30 08*

Paarl Wine Route
Wine route taking in the twenty best estates around Paarl. *Tel. 021/872-36 05*

MUSEUM

Paarl Museum
Exhibition about the architecture of the town. *303 Main St.; Mon–Fri 10 am–5 pm, Sat 10 am–12 pm*

RESTAURANT

Laborie
At this historical wine estate traditional Cape dishes are prepared. *Kohler St.; Tel. 021/807-33 90; category 3*

HOTELS

Lekkerwijn
This wonderful Cape Dutch farm house has belonged to the Pickstone family for generations. On the R 45 between Paarl and Franschhoek, *5 rms; Tel. + Fax 021/874-11 22; category 3*

Pontac Estate
This farm house dates back to 1723 and is one of the oldest in town. *15 rms; 16 Zion St.; Tel. 021/872-04 45; Fax 872-04 60; e-mail: pontac@iafrica.com; category 2*

INFORMATION

Tourist Information Bureau
216 Main St.; Mon–Fri 9 am–4 pm, Sat 9 am–12 pm; Tel. 021/872-38 29

SURROUNDING AREA

Le Bonheur Crocodile Farm (116/B5)
Over 1,000 crocodiles live on this farm. *Babylonstoren Rd.; Simondium; daily 10 am–5 pm*

PORT ELIZABETH

(119/D5) Although the British built a fort here as long ago as 1799, it was only in 1820 that a settlement was established in Port Elizabeth. The town was named after the wife of its founder, Sir Rufane Donkin. Elizabeth had died, two years before Donkin arrived in South Africa, at the age of 28. In South Africa the town is usually known simply as 'PE'.

The town (pop. 50,000) is of great significance economically. There is an important harbour and Port Elizabeth is also traditionally the centre of the South African automobile industry. Mercedes, Opel and Volkswagen have all constructed large manufacturing plants here. But there is much more to 'PE' than industry and the harbour — it is also a popular holiday destination. The town stretches for over 16 km along Algoa Bay and boasts some wonderful sandy beaches.

SIGHTS

Apple Express

This steam locomotive trundles along a narrow gauge track over 283 km from Port Elizabeth, through the fruit-growing region, to Loerie in Long Kloof. There is a wonderful view from the ◀▶ Van Staden River Bridge. *Humewood Station, Humewood Rd.; The train operates on average three times a month. Information: Tel. 041/507-23 33*

Campanile

◀▶ The tower commemorates the landing of the British settlers. It is 53 m high and affords a good view over the town. *At the entrance to the docks. The 23-bell carillon plays daily at 8.22 am, 1.32 pm and 6.02 pm. Mon, Tues, Thurs–Sat 9 am–1 pm and 2 pm–4 pm, Wed 8 am–12.30 pm*

Donkin Reserve

This park in the middle of the town was designated as 'a perpetual open space' by the founder of Port Elizabeth in 1820. A stone pyramid in the park commemorates Sir Rufane Donkin's wife with the inscription: 'She was one of the most perfect human beings who gave her name to the town'. *Belmont St.*

Snake Park

The snake park is housed in a complex, together with the *Oceanarium*, where there are dolphin and seal performances every day. In the *Tropical House* there are birds, reptiles and fish which live amongst tropical vegetation and in the *Night House*, nocturnal animals are housed in artificial moonlight. The snakes still have their poisonous fangs. They are 'milked' so that serum can be made from the poison. *Humewood Strand; daily 9 am–1 pm and 2 pm–5 pm; dolphin shows daily 11 am and 3 pm; admission approx. 4 R*

MUSEUMS

Port Elizabeth Museum

Besides the usual exhibitions about the history of the town, there is a part of the museum which is dedicated to the lives of the Xhosa tribes. In addition, there is a natural history section with stuffed animals. *Humewood Rd.; daily 9 am–5 pm*

Port Elizabeth: centre of the automobile industry and popular holiday destination

Cultural History Museum

The museum is housed on one of Port Elizabeth's oldest houses which was built in 1827. Displays include furniture of that period and a doll collection. *7 Castle Hill; Sun and Mon 2 pm–5 pm; Tues–Sat 10 am–1 pm and 2 pm–5 pm*

RESTAURANTS

Blackbeard's Lookout and Seafood Tavern

As implied by the name, this restaurant does not serve many meat dishes; the menu is dominated by seafood specialities. *Brooke's Pavilion, Beachfront; Tel. 041/55 55 67; category 1*

La Med

Mediterranean dishes are served here in a pleasant, relaxed atmosphere. *66a Parliament St.; Tel. 041/55 87 11; category 3*

Nelson's Arm

⚓ This old guest house has recently reopened. *3 Trinder Sq.; Tel. 041/56 00 72; category 2*

SHOPPING

Greenacres and the *Bridge Shopping Centre* in Cape Road are large shopping centres which sell everything imaginable.

HOTELS

Edward Hotel

☜ The Edward is located in the Old Town, at the Donkin Reserve. With a great view onto the harbour and town. *116 rms; Belmont Terrace; Tel. 041/56 20 56; Fax 56 49 25; category 3*

Hacklewood Hill

The owners of this country house specialise in elegance. *152 Prospect Rd., Walmer; Tel. 041/51 13 00; Fax 51 41 55; e-mail: pehotel@iaafrica.com; category 2*

SPORTS & LEISURE

Diving

There are plenty of ships in the waters around Port Elizabeth – a paradise for divers. Information

60

from *Ocean Divers International;
Tel. 041/55 27 23*

Deep-sea fishing
Information for deep-sea fishing enthusiasts is available from *Pro Dive Scuba; Tel. 041/583- 53 16.*

Windsurfing
Windsurfing equipment is available for rent on most beaches. *Tel. 041/55 24 80*

INFORMATION

Tourist Information
Donkin Lighthouse Building; Mon–Fri 8 am–3 pm, Sat 8.30 am–11.30 am; Tel. 041/55 88 84

SURROUNDING AREA

Addo Elephant Park (119/D4)
This national park is situated 72 km from Port Elizabeth. More than 200 elephants live in an area of around 9,000 hectares of bush. The elephants are protected after they almost became extinct in the 1920s. *The park is open all year round. The gates close every evening at 7 pm.* Not far from the Addo Elephant Park, on the banks of the Bushman's River, is the *Shamwari Game Reserve* where visitors who are not planning to visit the large game parks of the northern provinces can still have the opportunity to see the 'Big Five'. The hotel of the same name provides overnight accommodation. *35 rms; Summersand; Tel. 042/203- 11 11; Fax 235- 12 24; category 1*

Dias Cross (119/D5)
This is a replica of the cross which was erected by Bartholomeu Dias in 1488 in Kwaaihoek. *Kwaaihoek, near Beknes beach*

Mountain Zebra National Park (118/C3)
This national park is situated on the slopes of the Bankberg mountains. It was established in 1937 to safeguard the survival of the mountain zebras and seems to have been successful – in 1964 only 25 zebras existed but the figure has now risen to over 200. The park is also home to many other animals. Overnight accommodation is available in chalets. *Information Tel. 012/343 - 19 91*

St. Francis Bay (118/C5)
❖⤵‡The popular holiday resorts of St. Francis Bay, Cape St. Francis, Paradise Beach and Aston Bay are all located in a large bay. These isolated beaches are some of the best places for shell hunting. St. Francis Bay lies at the mouth of the Kromme River. From here it is possible to travel 12 km up river. This is a popular place for anglers. In the estuary area a canal system has been laid out with holiday cottages. The loveliest beach is the one which the surfers frequent. They claim this is where the most even, most perfect waves in the world are to be found. Indeed, this beach has been the venue for world championships. On the beach is the hotel *Cape St. Francis Holiday Resort, 30 cottages; Tel. 042/298- 00 54; Fax 298- 01 57; e-mail: scals@iafrica.com; category 3*

STELLENBOSCH

(116/B5) ★Stellenbosch is the second oldest town in South Africa (pop. 42,000). On one of his trips from Cape Town, Simon van der Stel was so taken with this valley that he decided to establish a settlement here. The town was founded in 1679 and was named after van der Stel. Walking through the oak-lined streets, it is easy to imagine that you have been transported back to the time Stellenbosch was founded. The town centre has been very well-preserved and in some places restoration work has been carried out. The wonderful Gothic church, the *Moederkerk*, was built in 1863. In the centre of the town there is a square with a large green area called *Die Braak* where parades were once held. The oldest and prettiest houses in Stellenbosch are built around Die Braak.

Stellenbosch became a university town in 1918 and has the most attractive university building in the country. This is *Victoria College* which was built in 1886. The area around Stellenbosch is called Boland. It is a magnificent landscape of mountains and fertile valleys. The lovely Cape Dutch houses are surrounded by vineyards. Many of them offer wine tasting to visitors as well as a light lunch.

SIGHTS

Bergkelder
Many of South Africa's particularly fine wines are produced here. *Guided tours through the wine cellars followed by wine tasting Mon–Sat at 10 am and 3 pm; Tel. 021/888- 30 16*

Dorp Street
The oldest street in Stellenbosch with the largest number of houses officially protected as historic monuments. Many of them date back to the 19th century. The Lutheran church, for example, was built in 1851 and now houses the university art gallery. Even some of the old oak trees in this street are protected by preservation orders.

MUSEUMS

Stellenryck Wine Museum
As well as looking round the wine museum, visitors can also see a collection of Cape Dutch furniture. *Dorp St.; Mon–Fri 9 am–12.45 pm, 2 pm–5 pm, Sat 10 am–1 pm*

Village Museum
The museum illustrates how the citizens of Stellenbosch lived between 1709 and 1850 in four houses dating from four different periods. The *Schreuderhuis*, built in 1710, was built by a German, Sebastian Schröder. It is the oldest townhouse in South Africa. The *Blettermanhuis* is furnished in the style of the period between 1760 and 1780. The neoclassical two-storey *Grosvenor House* represents the style of the first decade of the 19th century and *Bergh House* was the home of Marthinus Bergh and his family who lived here around 1850. *Ryneveld St.; Mon–Sat 9 am–5 pm, Sun 2 pm–5 pm*

RESTAURANTS

Die Volkskombuis
The restaurant is situated in a house which was designed by the famous architect, Herbert Baker. It serves traditional Cape cuisine in an authentic atmosphere. *Wagenweg; Tel. 021/887-21 21; category 3*

Delaire

◆◆ This charming estate advertises with the slogan 'vineyards in the clouds' and diners at the *Green Door* restaurant do indeed feel elevated here. *Helgshoogte Pass between Stellenbosch and Franschhoek. Tel. 021/885-17 56; category 2*

SHOPPING

Oom Samie Se Winkel

A traditional village shop typical of the last century. *84 Dorp St.*

HOTEL

D'Ouwe Werf

This establishment is one of South Africa's more traditional hotels. *25 rms; Church St.; Tel. 021/887-46 08; Fax 887-46 26; e-mail: ouwewerf@iafrica.com; category 3*

ENTERTAINMENT

Oude Libertas Centre

In the summer, operas, ballets and plays are performed in the open-air theatre. The audience comes prepared with blankets and picnic baskets. *Adam Tas Rd.; Tel. 021/808-74 74; Dec to April*

INFORMATION

Tourism and Information Bureau

36 Market St.; Mon–Fri 9 am–4 pm, Sat 8.30 am–12 pm; Tel. 021/ 883-35 84

SURROUNDING AREA

Meerlust (116/B5)

This wine estate is located between Cape Town and Stellenbosch. It has been owned by the Myburgh family for eight generations. The buildings are the most beautiful examples of Cape Dutch architecture. The best South African red wines are pressed here, as well as several Grappa varieties. Visits by prior arrangement only. *Tel. 021/843-35 87*

Stellenbosch Wine Route (116/B5)

❖ Over twenty wine estates within a 12-km radius of Stellenbosch have opened their gates to visitors. Information from *Stellenbosch Wine Route Office; 30 Plein St.; daily 9 am–5 pm; Tel. 021/ 886-43 10.* Visitors who do not wish to explore the wine route on their own are best advised to contact *Vineyard Ventures; Tel. 021/434-88 88; Fax 434-99 99*

Visit the wine estates in the area around Stellenbosch

Farmland in the heart of South Africa

Fields of wheat and maize, a walker's paradise and game parks on wide plateaux

The Orange Free State is surrounded by the northern provinces, KwaZulu-Natal and the Cape Provinces. While Natal is considered to be 'English', the Free State is 'Afrikaans'. The Boers who embarked on the Great Trek founded their Free State after they had crossed the Orange River during their flight from the British army. Winberg, the oldest town in the province, was founded in 1835. For the first few years, it was actually the capital of the Free State. The little town does not owe its name to winning a battle. In fact, the settlers were unable to decide to whom this land should belong. When one of the Boers finally won the argument, he called his estate Wenburg, meaning 'conquered fort'. Later it came to be written Winberg. Even today, it is still typical of the rural towns in Free State, being surrounded by vast plains and huge wheat and maize farms.

Lesotho – the independent 'kingdom in the sky' and home of the Basotho people

The respite from the British did not last long. In 1846, British officers came and bought Bloemfontein Farm which they wished to turn into a military base. Later the largest town in the Free State was founded on this site. At this point, many of the Boers set off again on a trek northwards, crossing the Vaal into Transvaal. Six years later, weary of the continual clashes, the British relinquished their claims on the region and accepted the establishment of an Orange Free State.

The province is situated on a high plateau. The land is to a large extent flat and covered in endless fields and grassland, but it is by no means lacking in contrast. In the east there are dramatic mountain ranges with peaks which are snow-topped in winter. The highland route between Harrismith in the north east and Zastron in the south provides a marvellous opportunity to experience the beauty of this region. The route leads through areas of spectacular views and landscapes and also boasts archaeological treasures, such as cave paintings left by prehistoric inhabitants. Bethlehem owes its name to the pious trekboers who, deeply impressed by the landscape, named it after the birthplace of Jesus. They also gave the river an equally Biblical name, Jordan. Not far away, at the foot of the Maluti Mountains is the *Golden Gate Highlands National Park* with spectacular sandstone formations and lots of animals.

Hidden away, high up in the mountains, is Qwa Qwa. The traditional home of the BaSotho people, Qwa Qwa is situated at an altitude of over 2,000 m. It is a fairytale land of high mountain peaks and gentle rolling grassland. Hikers will discover an area of incredible beauty here. BaSotho handicrafts are famous, especially the hand-woven woollen carpets which are sold in many shops all over South Africa.

In the north east of the Orange Free State is an area called the Riemland. This name came about when the settlers slaughtered thousands of the game herds which grazed on the wide plains.

The Boers then dried the skins and cut them up into narrow belts and sold them ('riem' means 'belt' or 'strap'). In the art gallery in Cape Town there is a picture which is entitled 'The greatest hunt of the century' which illustrates the excessive hunting which went on throughout the province. On one occasion in 1860, 4,000 antelopes were shot in one day, not far from Bloemfontein. The hunt took place in honour of Prince Alfred, son of Queen Victoria.

Nowadays, there are national parks and also a number of private game farms where animals such as the springbok, the national animal of South Africa, are again being reared. These farms can be recognised by the very high fences which are put up to protect the roads. In the middle of the province are the *gold fields,* which are 50 km long and 16 km wide. More than one third of South African gold is extracted in the area around Welkom. The first traces of this precious metal were found as early as 1903. However, it was not until thirty years later that prospecting began in earnest. The first attempts failed and the pioneers gave up, having suffered substantial losses. After World War II, the Anglo-American Corporation invested many millions of dollars into boring and geological investigations. Since that time, the area has become the centre of a modern mining industry. In Welkom, a new town which was built according to detailed plans, visitors can arrange to go and see one of the mines.

BLOEMFONTEIN

(113/F3) Bloemfontein is the capital of the Orange Free State (pop. 190,000) and is also the seat of the country's Supreme Court. The history of the town began back in 1840, when a Voortrekker called Nicolaa Brits came and decided to settle here. He named the town after the things which he discovered when he first arrived: a spring, *fontein,* surrounded by flowers, *bloem.*

Over the decades the town became a melting pot of Boer and British influences. The town is known as South Africa's rose city because of all its parks and gardens.

SIGHTS

First Raadsaal
The oldest building in Bloemfontein. Its thatched roof dates back to 1848 and was constructed on the orders of Major Warden who commanded the first British troops in the area. The building was the cradle of the government, the church and the educational system in the Free State. *St. Georges St.; Mon–Fri 10.15 am–3 pm; Sat and Sun 2 pm–5 pm*

Fontein
A pillar now is erected at the spot where the spring from which the town takes its name once bubbled up. *Selbourne Ave.*

Bloemfontein, capital of the Orange Free State

Bloemfontein, melting pot of Boer and British culture

Hamilton Park

★ One of the many old parks. The conservatory houses the largest orchid collection in South Africa. The atmosphere and watering of the more than 3,000 plants is controlled by a computer system. *Union Ave.; Mon–Fri 10 am– 4 pm, Sat and Sun 10 am–5 pm*

MUSEUM

National Museum

An enormous collection of fossils and a well-presented exhibition about the history of the Free State. *Aliwal St.; Mon–Sat 9 am– 4.30 pm, Sun 2 pm–5 pm*

RESTAURANT

Die Stalle

Traditional regional cuisine. Situated in the stables of the former president's residence. *President Brand St.; Tel. 051/430-34 23; category 3*

ACCOMMODATION

De Oude Kraal

This lovingly-restored farm hotel is situated 35 km outside Bloemfontein. *8 rms; on the N1 Riversford exit; Tel. 051/564-06 36; Fax 564-06 35; category 3*

Hobbit House

Lovingly-restored B&B in a Victorian House. Be sure to book in advance and enjoy the excellent meal which is served. *5 rms; 19 President Steyn Ave., Westdene; Tel. + Fax 051/447-06 63; category 3*

INFORMATION

Bloemfontein Information Bureau

President Brand St.; Mon–Fri 8 am– 4.15 pm, Sat 8 am–12 pm; Tel. 051/ 405-84 90

SURROUNDING AREA

Golden Gate Highlands National Park (107/F6)

★ ᔓᵛ The nature reserve takes its name from the fantastic sandstone cliffs which glisten like gold in the sunshine. This spectacular landscape covers an area of over 6,000 hectares and is home to many native animals. Eagles nest in the cliffs of the Maluti Mountains. There are two camps in the park where huts can be rented. *On the R 49 between Bethlehem and Harrismith; Tel. 012/343-19 91*

Lesotho (116/A2–B3–117/D1)

★ ᔓᵛ Independent kingdom in the middle of one of South Africa's mountain regions. Lesotho covers an area of 30,340 km^2 and is home to the Basotho who settled here at the beginning of the 19th century. In the capital, Maseru, there are good hotels, such as the *Maseru Sun with adjoining casino; 200 rms; Tel. 011/780-78 00 or 09266/31*

24 34; category 1. From here it is possible to go on excursions into the surrounding area. There are street markets selling Basotho handicrafts made from straw, such as *mokorotlo,* traditional pointed hats, and other craft articles. There are also top-quality hand-spun mohair woollen items.

Thaba Nchu (114/A1)

This little town was founded in 1873. It is the trading and administrative centre of the Tswana people. Situated at the foot of the Thaba Nchu Mountain, the village has a number of historic buildings and churches.

Not far from here is the *Thaba Nchu Sun,* a top-class hotel in the middle of a nature reserve. In the evenings, the guests can try their luck in the casino which is part of the hotel. *300 rms; Tel. 011/780-50 00; category 1*

Welkom (106/C5)

Welkom is the dynamic and throbbing heart of the gold fields which are among the richest in the world. The town was designed and laid out according to the plans of the former president of the Anglo-American Corporation, Sir Ernest Oppenheimer. It is divided into residential, industrial and mining areas, harmoniously linked by plenty of green areas. There are no traffic lights and only a few stop signs but there are over twenty roundabouts.

A visit to one of the gold mines is an exciting experience. Day trips should be booked in advance at the *Welkom Publicity Association; Tel. 057/352-92 44*

Welkom is a real paradise for birds. There are lots of small ponds in and around the town which provide habitats for large flocks of flamingos and many other species.

The Basotho people make carpets from their wool

Home of the Zulus

The province on the Indian Ocean
offers travellers a wide variety of activities

The beauty and diversity of the landscapes in KwaZulu-Natal are impressive, even though it is only a fairly small province. A wide range of different opportunities are available to people on holiday who choose to come here. There is the typically African bush in the north and the area of wide beaches on the Indian Ocean with its subtropical climate. There are green hills with rivers running through them and the most beautiful mountain range in the world, the *Drakensberg Mountains.*

The mixture of European, African and Asian cultures which is found here is fascinating. The largest section of the population is formed by the more than six million Zulus. Between 1820 and 1880, a large part of Natal was the Kingdom of Zululand. Many descendants of the famous warriors still live in this region today. Their reputation and that of their chiefs, Shaka and Dingaan, extends far beyond the country's borders. In 1816, at the age of 29, Shaka became chief of the Zulus. He was an illegitimate son of the old King. A combina-

tion of brutal determination and military genius had seen him rise quickly to the top in the army. Thus there was no question that Shaka would become the new King. He assembled an army of 60,000 warriors whom he continually sent out on campaigns. Other peoples were either defeated or they surrendered. Shaka trained his warriors to perfection and also developed new weapons and always rode at the front of an attack. His kingdom was bordered in the East by the Tugela River. Even the first settlers, British merchants who arrived from Cape Town in 1824, accepted this river as the border. Behind it they built a trade mission for the ships which passed through.

In 1838 the first trekboers arrived in Natal with their wagons pulled by oxen. By this time, Dingaan had killed his brother Shaka and had inherited his title. The Boers sent their leader, Piet Retief, to the new Zulu chieftain, Dingaan, to negotiate a peaceful co-existence. However, Retief's efforts were in vain and the whole delegation was murdered by the Zulus. They then attacked the Boers' main camp and killed several hundred people. They burned Port Natal to the ground

Zebras and impalas can be seen in Hluhluwe Game Reserve

71

and the inhabitants only managed to escape by taking refuge in ships off the coast. The Boers' revenge was terrible. At the Battle of Blood River, the white settlers completely destroyed the Zulu armies, in spite of the superior numbers of the latter. The Boers declared the area the Republic of Natalia, with Pietermaritzburg as the capital. However, this longed-for Boer republic did not last long. In 1843, Natal was declared a British colony and most of the Boers packed up their belongings and, disappointed, moved on once more. The wars between the British and the Zulus in 1879 and 1880 led to the final destruction of the once so great and powerful kingdom of the Zulus. Yet many traditions have survived. When travelling through Zululand today, time seems to have stood still. There are kraals where the tribal lifestyle continues today much as it has done for centuries.

The climate is ideal for the cultivation of tropical plants and fruits. In the middle of the last century, settlers planted sugarcane. This was very successful, as can be seen today by the huge plantations and estates. Since the Zulus did not want to work in the fields and slavery was prohibited, immigrant workers were brought over from India. They came from the lowest castes and were often pleased to be able to find work in Natal.

The KwaZulu-Natal coast is a holiday paradise. Fantastic beaches with numerous holiday resorts extend to the north and south of Durban. The largest and most popular holiday destination is Durban itself. But the other resorts also have something for every taste. Visitors can find peace and quiet in the little villages and fun and entertainment in larger places, such as Margate and Unhlanga. And the Drakensberg Mountains boast magnificent scenic landscapes.

MARCO POLO SELECTION: KWAZULU-NATAL

1 Indian markets in Durban
A fascinating blend of Asia and Africa
(page 74)

2 Valley of a Thousand Hills
There are wonderful views from the many gently rolling hills
(page 76)

3 Umhlanga Rocks
Popular holiday resort on the Indian Ocean
(page 76)

4 Eshowe
One of the oldest towns in Zululand. A replica village was built here for the filming of the TV series, Shaka Zulu. It is now a hotel (page 75)

5 Drakensberg Mountains
The Alps of South Africa and the beautiful surrounding landscape are popular with mountain climbers and hikers from all over the world (page 77)

They stretch from the eastern Cape to the north east of the country and are also known as the Alps of South Africa. One of the highest peaks in this range is the *Mont aux Sources* (3,299 m) which received its name from the five rivers which rise here. The best-known of these is the Tugela. Immense cliffs form an amphitheatre which is eight kilometres long. It is part of the *Royal Natal National Park*, an area of incredibly beautiful landscapes and lots of rare flowers and animals, especially birds of prey. It is only one of many national parks for the protection of plants and animals in Natal. *Umfolozi* was set up to protect rhinoceroses. The *Mkuzi Park* was established in 1912. It lies at the foot of the *Ubombo Mountains* and is home to many species, including leopards, giraffes, rhinoceroses, zebras and hippos.

DURBAN

(115/F2) With its broad white beaches on the Indian Ocean, Durban is a real mecca for people on holiday in South Africa. The sun shines 300 days a year. Arriving today in this large, throbbing harbour town, it is impossible to imagine that 150 years ago there was nothing here but jungle with lions and elephants. The Zulus still call the city *Ethekwini*, meaning the peaceful lagoon.

Vasco da Gama saw this heavenly land for the first time at the end of 1497 on his way to Asia. As it was Christmas, he called it Natal, meaning nativity. It was only in 1835 that the settlers changed the name to Dur-ban, after Sir D'Urban who was Governor of the Cape at the time.

The city (pop. 1,100,000) is a fascinating mixture of so many different cultures and peoples. Half of the inhabitants are descendants of the Indian workers brought here by the British colonial powers to the sugar-cane plantations. The Indian markets, mosques and shops are among the greatest attractions of Durban.

The harbour is the largest in the country, in terms both of area and of volume. More freight is handled here than in any other harbour in the continent.

SIGHTS

Harbour tours/sea trips

Harbour tours and pleasant cruises for those who enjoy life on the ocean wave start from the Pleasure Cruise Terminal at the harbour. *Sarie Marais Jetty; Tel. 031/305-4022*

Juma Mosque

This mosque is the largest and most magnificent in the Southern Hemisphere. Definitely well worth a visit. *Corner of Grey St. and Queen St.*

Natal Shark Board

There are lots of sharks off the coast of Natal. More than 300 nets have been set up to keep them away from the beaches. The research institute examines the 1,000 sharks which are caught every year. *On a hill above Umhlanga*

Rickshaw stands

❖ Zulus in traditional costume offer rickshaw rides along the promenade at South Beach.

Sea World

Here visitors can see sharks at close quarters. In addition, there are over one thousand species of fish living in various pools, the largest of which holds 820,000 litres of sea water. Just nearby is the dolphinarium. *Daily 9 am–4.30 pm (last admission); shows at 10 am, 11.30 am, 2 pm, 3 pm and 5 pm. Feeding time at 11 am and 3 pm. Corner of West Parade and Marine Parade; admission approx. 15 R*

Umgeni River Bird Park

Park with exotic birds from all over the world. *Marine Parade across the Umgeni River Bridge; daily 9 am–4.30 pm; admission approx. 9 R*

MUSEUM

Local History Museum

Clothes, furniture and other items from the early days of Durban are displayed here in this old courthouse. *Aliwal St., Mon–Sat 9 am–5 pm; Sun 11 am–5 pm*

RESTAURANTS

Café Fish

↘↗❄ The restaurant is situated right on the harbour. *Yachtmole; Tel. 031/305-5062; category 2*

Gulzar

For those who enjoy Indian cuisine, the best place. Wonderful atmosphere. *69 Stamford Hill Rd., Morningside; Tel. 031/309-63 79; category 2*

Le St. Geran

This restaurant, furnished in pink, is one of the ten best in the country. *Florida Rd.; Tel. 031/303-2630; category 1*

SHOPPING

African Art Centre

❖ Original artwork and handicrafts by Zulu artists is displayed and sold here. *35 Guildhall Arcade, Gardiner St.; Mon–Fri 9 am–5 pm, Sat 9 am–1 pm*

Durban: both a mecca for holiday-makers and a commercial metropolis

Indian markets

★❄ An absolute must for visitors to Durban. 180 different booths in *Victoria Street* sell spices, fish, meat, jewellery and much more.

There are similar booths in the *Oriental Arcades.* Here street traders sell jewellery, silk, saris shot with gold thread and other items. It is acceptable and expected for customers to haggle with the vendors. *Victoria St. and*

Oriental Arcade between Crey Rd. and Cathedral Rd.; closed Sun

Pavillion

This shopper's paradise is situated 15 minutes outside the city centre on the N 3 in the direction of Pietermaritzburg. Secure carparks and security police.

HOTELS

Holiday Inn Crown Plaza

↘ This large hotel is to be recommended for its spectacular views over the Indian Ocean. *444 rms; Snell Parade; Tel. 031/37 13 21; Fax 32 55 27; category 2*

Quarter's Hotel

Superbly-run hotel which is not too large. The guests are provided with fresh flowers and home-made biscuits in their attractive rooms. *25 rms; 101 Florida Rd., Morningside; Tel. 031/303-52 46; Fax 303-52 66; e-mail: quarter@lcon.co.za; category 1*

The Royal

A top hotel in the city centre which achieves the perfect combination of colonial atmosphere and modern hotel comfort. *272 rms; 267 Smith St.; Tel. 031/304-03 31; Fax 307-68 86; category 1*

SPORTS & LEISURE

Sailing, surfing and windsurfing

❂ Everything's possible. Surfing: *Tel. 031/37 40 38,* Windsurfing: *Tel. 031/22 41 59,* Sailing: *Tel. 031/657-26*

Water Wonderland

For watersports enthusiasts. *Snell Parade; 031/32 97 76*

ENTERTAINMENT

Golden Mile

⚚❂ Pleasure and entertainment are found in great abundance on the Golden Mile, which actually extends for six kilometres along the promenade. Hotels, bars and restaurants are found side-by-side. At the *Natal Playhouse* all sorts of performances are put on, ranging from opera and cabaret. *Promenade*

INFORMATION

Tourist Junction

160 Pine St.; Mon–Fri 8 am–5 pm, Sat and Sun 9 am–2 pm; Tel. 031/304-49 34

SURROUNDING AREA

Dingaan's Kraal (Umgungundlovu) (109/D5)

This is the spot where the leader of the Boers, Piet Retief, and his men were killed by the Zulu chieftain, Dingaan, in 1838. The kraal was reconstructed and is now a museum. *On the R 34 towards Vryheid*

Eshowe (115/F1)

★ Eshowe is one of the oldest places in Zululand. The television series about Shaka Zulu was filmed at the *Hotel Shakaland.* A replica Zulu village was built for the filming and was later converted into a hotel. *Tel. 035/460-08 12; Fax 460-08 24; category 2*

Hluhluwe Game Park (109/E4–5)

Lying at the foot of the mountains, this nature reserve boasts a unique combination of landscapes; forest, savannah and grassland. Black and white rhinoceroses, elephants, buffaloes, zebras, lions, leopards and many other animals all live here.

Accommodation is provided in luxury ❧ treehouses which are connected by wooden walkways. The view is fantastic. *Tel. 035/562-01 44; Fax 562-02 05; category 2.* Visitors can go on safari at any of the three nearby game reserves – *Hluhluwe, Umfolozi* and *Mkuzi.* Only 8 km away is the private game reserve, *Bushland Game Lodge. Near Mkuzi* is the *Phinda Tzilwane* game reserve where attempts are being made to reintroduce the species which lived here in the past, such as elephants and lions. Farmland is also being returned to wilderness. Phinda is Zulu for 'return'. *42 rms; Tel. 011/803-84 21; Fax 803-18 10*

Kwabulawayo (109/D6)
The only evidence today of Shaka's capital is a monument. Not far from here there is a small hotel where guests can spend the night in the style of the sugar barons. *Mine Own Country House, Gingindhlovul; 5 rms; Tel. 035/ 337-12 62; Fax 337-10 25; category 3*

Valley of a Thousand Hills (115/E2)
★ ❧ From Botha Hill there is a spectacular view over the hills and valleys. In the early morning, before the mist has lifted, the cries of the Zulus can sometimes be heard as they pass on their news from hill to hill. 500 m below the *Rob Roy Hotel*, there is a kraal where the Zulus perform their dances. Witch doctors foretell the future from bones thrown onto the ground. *37 rms; Rob Roy Hotel; Bothas Hill;*

Tel. 031/ 777-13 05; Fax 777-13 64; category 3

Umhlanga Rocks (115/F2)
★ A particularly lovely holiday destination on the shores of the Indian Ocean. Besides excellent spots for bathing, a visit to *Croc World,* a crocodile farm, is highly recommended. (*93 rms; Tel. 031/561-22 33; Fax 561-40 72; category 2).* The hotels are situated right on the beach. One of the best is the *Oyster Box.* As the name implies, the oysters here are particularly scrumptious.

A really heavenly place to stay is found 30 km further on in *Umhlali* at the ❧ *Zimbali Lodge.* Above the Dolphin Coast, surrounded by beautiful forest, the hotel boasts luxury bedrooms, first-class food and its own 18-hole golf course. *76 rms; Tel. 011/ 780-78 00; Fax 780-74 44; category 1*

PIETERMARITZBURG

(**115/E2**) Pietermaritzburg (pop. 170,000) is surrounded by green hills and is located in a wide valley. The old town centre, with its Victorian houses, reflects the influence of the British colonial period. However, the town was founded by the trekboers who settled here after the Battle of Blood River. They founded the Republic of Natalia and named their capital after the two leaders, Piet Retief and Gerrit Maritz.

SIGHTS

Howick Falls
Here the Umgeni River plunges down 111 m. *On the road to Ho-*

wick in the Umgeni Valley Nature Reserve

Voortrekker House

This is the only house which has survived since the time of the pioneers. *333 Boom St.; Mon–Fri 9 am–5 pm, Sun 9 am–12.30 pm*

MUSEUMS

Macrorie House Museum

The museum has a collection of Victorian furniture which belonged to early British settlers. *Corner of Pine St. and Loop St.; Tues–Thurs 9 am–4 pm*

Voortrekker Museum

Collection of keepsakes from the time of the pioneers. *340 Church St.; Mon–Fri 9 am–1 pm and 2 pm–4.30 pm, Sat 8 am–12 pm*

RESTAURANTS

Didier's Hotel

Classic French cuisine by one of the best chefs in the region. *Hilton Hotel, Hilton Rd.; Tel. 0331/43 33 59; category 2*

Turtle Bay

❖ There's always something happening here. Specially recommended: ostrich and pistachio tureens. *Wembley Terrace; Tel. 0331/94 53 90; category 3*

HOTELS

Imperial Hotel

A grand old hotel. It is named after Prince Louis Napoleon, the Imperial Crown Prince, who stayed here, before going off to fight in the Zulu War where in 1879, at the age of 23, he was killed. *43 rms; 224 Loop St.; Tel.*

0331/42 65 51; Fax 42 97 96; category 2

Rawdons Hotel

Idyllically nestled in the countryside in the little village of *Nottingham Road. 37 rms; Tel./Fax 0333/360-44; category 3*

INFORMATION

Tourist Information Bureau

177 Commercial Rd.; Mon–Fri 8.30 am–4.30 pm, Sat 8.30 am–12.30 pm; Tel. 0331/45 13 48

SURROUNDING AREA

Drakensberg Mountains (115/D1–2)

★ ☙ The view of the amphitheatre in the *Royal Natal National Park* is unforgettable. In many of the caves in this area, there are paintings by the bushmen who for centuries sought shelter here. In the *Giant's Castle Nature Reserve* there is a *museum devoted to the bushman paintings. Daily 11.30 am–2.30 pm.* In order to appreciate this natural wonder to the full, visitors are recommended to stay in one of the many hotels which offer great views. *Cathedral Peak Hotel; 90 rms; Tel./Fax 036/488-18 88; e-mail: chp@ls.lia.net; category 3,* and *Champagne Castle Hotel; 49 rms; Tel. 036/468-10 63; Fax 468-13 06; category 3*

Midmar Nature Reserve (108/C6)

There are lots of opportunities for water sports enthusiasts at this lake. In *Midmar Historical Village,* an open-air museum, visitors can see how the people of Natal used to live. *Currently only open on Sundays*

Land of gold and diamonds

The region previously known as the Transvaal is now divided into the Northern, Gauteng, Mpumalanga and North-West Provinces

When visitors arrive in the morning at the Jan Smuts Airport in Johannesburg, they experience something of Africa straight away: the clear, dry air of the highveld, a vast reddish-coloured landscape of high grassland plateaux and the breathtakingly beautiful sunrises of the north. This was the last part of the country to be settled by the whites. The industrial metropolis of Johannesburg is just over 100 years old and Pretoria is only a few decades older. The capital's founder, Wesel Pretorius, named the city after his father who was one of the Boer generals at the Battle of Blood River. After the proclamation of the free province of Transvaal in 1854, the country which is now South Africa comprised two British colonies, the Cape and Natal, and the Boer Republics of Transvaal and the Orange Free State. With the discovery of diamonds in Transvaal, the British attempted to

The 'Three Rondavels' at Blyde River Canyon, in the Drakensberg Mountains in eastern Transvaal

persuade the Boers into a confederation. When this failed they annexed the Republics which resulted in the First Anglo-Boer War which is still referred to in Afrikaans as *Vryheidsoorlog,* the 'freedom war'. The Boers won and in 1881 Transvaal regained its independence. The country developed under the leadership of the legendary President Paul 'Ohm' Kruger. When extensive gold reserves were discovered not far from Pretoria in 1886, he realised the problems which could arise as a result. However, it was impossible to keep the finds secret. The gold rush which subsequently erupted attracted thousands of adventurers from all over the world to the region.

After the gold discoveries, Britain was even more determined to incorporate this part of southern Africa into the crown colony. This led to the Second Anglo-Boer War. In 1902 the Boers were forced to admit defeat. In 1910 the Union of South Africa was founded with Pretoria as the administrative capital.

Gold was discovered in the Witwatersrand plateau which

lies at an average altitude of 1,700 m above sea level. The vein of gold extends over 130 km and is 30 km wide at its end. There are many mining and industrial towns which have grown up in this area, the largest of which is, of course, Johannesburg. The Vaal River is very popular amongst the Johannesburgers as a destination for weekend trips. Visitors can stay in attractive hotels or rent cottages or houses.

The university town of Potchefstrom, founded in 1838, was the first capital of the South African Republic. Many buildings still evoke that past today.

North of Pretoria is the beginning of the *Great North Road.* The Great North Road leads through hilly bushveld to Warmbad. The town is famous for its hot springs which are particularly beneficial to people who suffer from rheumatism.

From here the drive continues via Waterberg and Pietersburg through the Baobab Plains and the Soutpansberg and finally, after hundreds of kilometres to the Limpopo. The river forms the border with Zimbabwe and Botswana. The drive is a great experience for Africa lovers.

The most well-known and interesting of the northern provinces is Mpumalanga. Its history is full of adventures and dramatic events. The settlers had already found gold here, before the rush began in Witwatersrand. *Pilgrim's Rest,* now a ghost town and a tourist attraction, was one of the towns associated with the beginning of the gold rush. Some of the old gold mines are still operating. How-

Traces of the gold rush can be seen all over the country

ever, the main source of income has long been agriculture, particularly the cultivation of subtropical fruit. There are plenty of impressive vantage points from which to view the bizarre countryside and mighty waterfalls. Here in Mpumalanga the inland plateau drops off to the subtropical level 1,000 m below. It is a dramatic landscape, the high lights of which can be seen along the *Panorama Route* .

It is a good idea to allow plenty of time for a visit to *Kruger Park* . The park is one of the most famous game reserves in the world. Overnight accommodation is available in camps in the park. In addition, there are a number of private game farms which have been established along the western boundary of Kruger Park, where experienced gamekeepers lead guests on safari.

JOHANNESBURG

(107/E3) Johannesburg is situated an impressive 1,753 m above sea-level. It is built on gold in the truest sense of the word and enjoys more days of sunshine than California. Even in winter, though the nights are cold, the days are still warm. It is the largest city in South Africa. If the population of the city (1.9 million) is added to that of the townships of Soweto, then there are more than four million people living in the metropolis of Johannesburg. Added to that are the shanty towns on the outskirts of the city.

As far as its geographical location is concerned, Johannesburg cannot compete with Cape Town. Yet it still holds its own, very different fascination. The atmosphere is buzzing and the lifestyle fast, exciting and sometimes reckless, as in the early days of the city. Everything revolves around money and business. Jo-

hannesburg is South Africa's trade and financial centre, with the stock exchange, the largest airport, the widest streets and the highest skyscrapers in the country. From the view point in the Carlton Centre, the outlook over the glittering skyline certainly conveys a vision of the beating pulse of South Africa's economy. Over its one-hundred-year history Johannesburg has been rebuilt three times. Land prices in the city centre are now so high as to make it worthwhile to demolish old buildings and build new, higher ones. There are two universities.

In the African languages, Johannesburg is called *E'Goli,* meaning 'City of Gold' because it all began with gold. In 1886 George Harrison, an Australian sculptor, who had already looked for gold in his own country, came here on his way to the eastern Transvaal and noticed the gold content of the stone. What followed has

MARCO POLO SELECTION: NORTHERN PROVINCES

1 Gold Reef City
Replica of a gold-digging town in Johannesburg with hotels and bars (page 82)

2 African Herbalist Shop
Medicine men and women sell miracle cures and herbs (page 83)

3 Sun City and Lost City
Luxury pleasure complex with hotels, casinos, sports facilities and much more (page 84)

4 Union Building
Government building in Pretoria, surrounded by a sea of jacaranda blossoms beginning in October (page 85)

5 Tzaneen
Situated in a beautiful valley in the north (page 88)

6 Kruger Park
Probably the most beautiful, certainly the most famous game reserve in the world (page 87)

gone down in history as the largest gold rush of all time. Gold-diggers from three continents set out on the arduous journey. In those days, the trip from the coast into the centre of the country was an adventure in itself. Johannesburg, where gold still plays a major role today, grew out of a camp with tents and makeshift huts erected by the gold-diggers.

SIGHTS

☞ City Map on pages 120/121

Goldmines (O)

A trip to a goldmine can be booked through the South African Chamber of Mines. Visitors can go down into the mines and watch as pure molten gold is poured into an ingot. Those under sixteen and over sixty years of age are not usually allowed to make the underground trip. To make the visit worthwhile, it is advisable to allow a whole day for it. On Sundays workers perform traditional dances at some goldmines. *Bookings Tel. 011/ 838-8211*

Gold Reef City (O)

★ Since no buildings had survived since the time of the gold rush, this authentic town was built to recreate the atmosphere of that time. There are replicas of various buildings, including houses, a newspaper printworks, a brewery, a theatre, a bank, a fire station and a hotel.

Visitors can go on tours around Gold Reef City in a little train or in carriages. It is also possible to go down a mine shaft to explore the old goldmines beneath the town. The adjacent

funfair has some thrilling rides. *Crown district; 15 minutes from the city centre; buses depart from the Hotel Sandton Sun and from the city hotels, operated by Horizon Tours, Tel. 011/496-1600.*

Gold Reef City

Lion Park (O)

Here visitors can drive among the lions as they wander freely about the park. *30 km from Johannesburg on the R 512 towards Lanseria airport; daily 8 am–5 pm; admission 15 R*

Soweto (O)

South Western Townships. More than two million people live in this predominantly black suburb. In 1976, Soweto became world famous when demonstrations by schoolchildren ended in bloodshed. *Information on tours from Jimmy's face to face Tours; Tel. 011/331-6109*

MUSEUMS

Geological Museum (120/C4–5)

A very extensive exhibition of minerals and a unique collection of gold nuggets and ores. *Corner of Sauer St. and President St.;*

Mon–Sat 9 am–5.30 pm, Sun 2 pm–5.30 pm

Johannesburg Art Gallery (121/D3)
An international art collection and works by South African painters are displayed. *Jourbert Park; Tues–Sun 10 am–5 pm*

Museum Africa (120/B4)
Exhibitions illustrating life in southern Africa from the Stone Age to apartheid. *121 Bree St.; Tues–Sun 9 am–5 pm*

Museum of Military History (O)
Includes an exhibition on the military arm of the ANC. *Jan Smuts Ave.; opposite the airport; 9 am–4.30 pm*

RESTAURANTS

Casalinga (O)
Situated a little out of the city but in a beautiful location near the Rocky Ridge Golf Course. *Tel. 011/957-26 12; category 1*

Gramadoelas at the Market (120/B4)
A restaurant which serves the whole range of South African cuisine. *Corner of Bree St. and Wolhuter St.; Tel. 011/838-69 60; category 2*

Zoo Lake (O)
The restaurant is situated in the same park as the zoo and offers pleasant views. *Jan Smuts Ave.; Tel. 011/646-88 07; category 1*

HOTELS

The Grace in Rosebank (O)
Centrally located hotel with an unusual swimming pool. *60 rms; 54 Bath Ave..; Tel. 011/ 280-72 00; Fax 280-74 74; e-mail: thegrace@grace.co.za; category 2*

Fairlawns (O)
The large rooms are sumptuously decorated. *11 rms; Alma Rd.; Morningside Manor; Tel. 011/ 804-25 40; Fax 802-72 61; e-mail: anna@fairlawns.co.za; category 1*

Maweni (O)
The first guest house in Soweto boasts a sauna, a steam bath and a swimming pool. *In Protea Glenn district. 3 rms; Tel. 011/986-11 42; category 3*

The Westcliff (120/B1)
Orient Express Hotel. Situated in the most elegant suburb of Johannesburg, it opened at the beginning of 1997. *64 rms; 67 Jan Smuts Ave.; Tel. 011/ 23 10 50; Fax 23 10 60; e-mail: nellress@iaafrica.com; category 1*

SHOPPING

African Herbalist Shop (120/B4)
★Sells African herbs. A consultation with a native medicine man or woman is possible. *14 Diagonal St.*

African Rooftop Market (O)
Everything from junk to antiques is sold *every Sunday in the Rosebank Mall between 9.30 am and 5 pm* at approx. 450 different booths. *50 Bath Ave.*

Hyde Park Corner (O)
Small but very exclusive shopping centre. *Hyde Park*

Sandton City (O)
The largest and most impressive shopping centre. Shop after shop with everything you could

possibly wish to buy. *In Sandton district*

ENTERTAINMENT

Razzmatazz

This is where the trendy people go. *Corner of Claim St. and Smit St.*

Market Theatre   (120/B4)

🏃 ❀ ✪ The Market Theatre has four stages. This is where the best productions in South Africa are performed. The well-known musical 'Sarafina' was first performed here. In addition, the area also boasts a book shop, an art gallery, a bar and a restaurant. Then there is the artists' centre, housed in the old market halls which date back to 1913. Nearby there are many other small alternative shops and galleries. *Wolhuter St.; Tel. 011/832-16 41*

INFORMATION

Johannesburg Publicity Association   (121/D4)

Corner of Market St. and Kruis St.; Mon–Thurs 8 am–4.30 pm, Fri 8 am–4 pm, Sat and Sun 8 am–1 pm; Tel. 011/336-49 61

SURROUNDING AREA

Hartbeespoort Dam   (107/E2)

The reservoir lies in the Magaliesberg Mountains, between Johannesburg and Pretoria. The aquarium which houses crocodiles, seabirds and seals is well worth a visit and just next to it there is a snake park. Balloon trips over the dam operate daily, weather permitting. *Tel. 012 05/510-21.* Not far from the reservoir there is a research centre where leopards, cheetahs and

other rare animals are bred. *Wild Cheetah Centre, Tel. 012/504-19 21*

Sun City and Lost City   (107/D1)

★ This vast entertainment complex is a two-and-a-half-hour drive from Johannesburg. It appears from the middle of the dry bush landscape like an oasis in the desert. The hotel complex and its casinos are situated in an extinct volcanic crater of the Pilansberg Mountains. In the three hotels, *The Cascades, Sun City and Cabanas,* the guests are truly spoiled. Each hotel has several swimming pools and many other sports facilities. There is a huge lake where visitors can enjoy all sorts of water sports. The 18-hole golf course was laid out by Gary Player. In parts of the

Sun City, a real oasis of pleasure

park it is easy to imagine that you are in the jungle. Yet everything is artificial. Before Sun City was built, there were no waterfalls, no palm trees, no flamingos or parrots. In the evening visitors can choose between numerous *restaurants,* the *casino,* the *arcade games* and *shows* of international repute. There is also the opportunity to go on safaris in the nearby Pilansberg National Park. Five years ago a 26-hectare extension to this hotel and pleasure complex was opened. The 'Lost City', with its *Hotel Palace,* appears like a mirage. This fairy tale world is a combination of Indian palace and jungle, with huge waterfalls, artificial lakes and a desert golf course. The whole complex is supposed to evoke images of a long-lost civilisation where visitors become caught in a dream world. *Sun City is equipped with a railway station and an airport. There are daily flights to Sun City from Johannesburg. The Sun City Express takes visitors who have come for the day from the carpark to the various entertainments. Buses depart daily from Johannesburg; Tel. 011/780 - 78 00 or 014651/2100.*

Wonder Cave (107/E2)

This limestone cave is over two billion years old. It is among the most impressive natural features in South Africa. *Daily 8 am–5 pm; guided tours every ninety minutes from 8 am. Beyond Randburg on the R 47; admission 6 R*

PRETORIA

(**107/E2**) The Union Building in Pretoria (pop. one million) stands in splendour above the city. When the Parliament is not sitting in Cape Town, the country is governed from here. The seat of government was built by the famous architect, Sir Herbert Baker, after the establishment of the Union of South Africa in 1910. Nelson Mandela's inauguration took place in the imposing Union Building with its 2,000-seat amphitheatre. It is surrounded by a beautiful park and the residences of ministers and ambassadors.

The difference between the two neighbouring cities of Johannesburg and Pretoria could not be more pronounced. The first is lively and cosmopolitan, the second is peaceful and reserved. In October, the city is transformed by a sea of flowers when 70,000 jacaranda trees bathe the city in a lilac glow.

SIGHTS

National Zoological Garden

↯ With 3,500 species of animals, the zoo is one of the largest in the world. A special cable car takes visitors to view points far above the animal enclosures. *Paul Krüger St.; daily 8 am–6 pm; admission approx. 7.50 R*

Union Building

★ The seat of government is situated on the Meintjieskop. It is viewed upon by many as a masterpiece of South African architecture. In 1994, on the steps of the building, Nelson Mandela took his oath of office.

Voortrekker Monument

This massive granite monument commemorates the terrible Battle of Blood River. In the Hall of Heroes 27 marble panels depict the story of the Great Trek. *Fontains Valley; Mon–Sat 9 am–4.45 pm, Sun 11 am–4.45 pm*

MUSEUM

Transvaal Museum

This museum displays geological and archaeological discoveries

The Union Building stands in splendour above Pretoria

and fossils, including artefacts of the prehistoric peoples of the region. *Paul Krüger St.; Mon–Sat 9 am–5 pm, Sun 11 am–5 pm*

RESTAURANTS

Chagall's
Situated in the middle of a park. Leisurely atmosphere, good food. *924 Park St., Arcadia; Tel. 012/342-12 00; category 1*

La Madeleine
This has been the Number 1 restaurant in Pretoria for many years. *Esselen St., Sunnyside; Tel. 012/44 60 76; category 1*

Die Werf
Traditional Afrikaans cuisine in a traditional Afrikaans atmosphere. *Olympus Dr.; Tel. 012/991-18 09; category 3*

SHOPPING

Bushman Shop
A great place to find original souvenirs. *Central St.*

HOTELS

Mount Grace
One of the most attractive country hotels in the area. *65 rms; Magaliesburg; Tel. 014/577-13 50; Fax 577-12 02; e-mail: mntgrace@iafrica.com; category 2*

Victoria Hotel
This hotel, built in 1896, has been lovingly and painstakingly restored to its old glory by the Rovos Rail Group. *28 rms; Corner of Scheiding/Paul Krüger St.; Tel. 012/323-60 52; Fax 012/323-08 43; category 1*

INFORMATION

Tourist Rendezvous Centre
Vermeulen St.; daily 8 am–5 pm; Tel. 012/308-89 37

SURROUNDING AREA

Crocodile River
Arts and Crafts Ramble   (107/E2)
Drive to the Magaliesberg Mountains, then towards Ho-

neydew. Along the route, famous South African artists have their studios which are open the first weekend of every month for the public to browse and buy.

Cullinan Mine (107/E2)
It was in this diamond mine that the 3,106 carat Cullinan was found – the largest diamond in the world. *Premier Diamond Mine, Cullinan; along the R 513; Tel. 01213/400-81; guided tours Tues– Fri 9.30 am and 11 am; no admission for children under ten*

Kruger Park (103/E–F1–6)
★ The world-famous, two-million-hectare game park is home to the widest diversity of animals on the African continent. Access to the park is gained by eight different gates, four of which can be reached from *Nelspruit: Malelane, Crocodile Bridge, Numbi* and the *Paul Kruger Gate.* The park can be entered in the middle at *Orpen* and *Phalabora,* and in the north are the entrances *Punda Maria* and *Pafuri.* Overnight accommodation is available in round huts or small houses in the camps. The smaller camps are self-catering, whereas the larger ones, such as *Pretoriuskop* and *Berg-en-Dahl,* have *restaurants* and *swimming pools.*

In South Africa the importance and significance of conservation was recognised at an early stage. At the end of the last century, the government of the time made the decision to ban hunting between the Sabie and Crocodile Rivers. Thus, the Kruger National Park was established. There are 130 species of mammals, 48 fish, 115 reptile and 468 bird species living in the beautiful landscape of this park. The park authorities estimate that there are 8,000 elephants, 26,000 buffaloes and 120,000 impalas, as well as zebras, lions, leopards, cheetahs, giraffes, hippos, rhinoceroses and many others species besides.

Visitors can drive through the park on very good roads and watch the animals. The speed limit on asphalt roads is 50 km/h and on the sandy tracks it is 40 km/h. *Oct–Mar 5.30 am–6 pm, Apr–Sept 6 am–5.30 pm. Information and reservations: National Parks Board; Tel. 012/343-19 91; Fax 343-20 00; category 3*

Mala Mala/Rattray, Londolozi and Sabi Sabi Game Reserves (103/F4–5)
On the western border of Kruger Park there are also a number of private game reserves. In terms of animals they are very similar to Kruger Park, although they are much smaller. Accommodation tends to be much more luxurious and also more expensive. Game keepers drive through the bush with visitors in four-wheel drive vehicles to ensure that, even in a few hours, as many animals as possible can be sighted. It is almost always *The Big Five,* that is lions, elephants, buffaloes, rhinoceroses and leopards, which are seen.

The private parks also offer the opportunity to go on night safari, something which is not allowed in Kruger Park. On hot days especially the animals tend to be lethargic, so the exciting things happen at night.

Mala Mala/Rattray Reserve is the largest and the oldest of South Africa's game reserves. It covers an area of 18,000 hectares and shares a 30-km-long border with the Kruger National Park. Mala Mala is renowned for seeking to indulge the visitor's every whim. The accommodation is first-class and very luxurious, as are the safaris and the food. For guests who wish to go on safari on foot, there are 'Trekker Trails' with accommodation provided in luxury tents. *Various camps in different price ranges. But: all category 1. Tel. 011/789-26 77; Fax 886-43 82*

Londolozi Game Reserve: Accommodation here is in three camps along the Sand River. It may not be quite as luxurious but it is still noble and fairly expensive. �™The *Tree Camp* is built round an old ebony tree and affords a wonderful panoramic view. *Tel. 011/784-70 77; Fax 784-76 67; category 1*

Sabi Sabi Game Reserve borders on the Kruger Park too. Here visitors are also accompanied by ranchers. In the evenings, barbecued game is served under Africa's magnificent starry sky. *Tel. 011/483-39 39; Fax 483-37 99; e-mail: com@sabisabi.com; category 1*

Mpumalanga (103/F3–109/D3)

The majority of the province is subtropical with fertile plains. Approaching via the ☙Panorama Route, the view of its forests and bush is wonderful. It was only with incredible effort and determination that the Voortrekkers managed to cross the mountains with their ox-wagons. Later, when gold was discovered, in *Barberton,* for example, gold-diggers came too. As the gold deposits were exhausted fairly quickly, Barberton remained a dreamy little town, rather than becoming a metropolis like Johannesburg.

Sabie (103/E5)

The town of forests and waterfalls. The waterfalls are the *Mac Mac Falls* from where the route over Graskop leads to the *Blyde River Canyon,* surely one of the most impressive places in South Africa. The best view point is at ☙God's Window which is only 15 km from Graskop. Not far from Sabie is *Pilgrim's Rest,* a picturesque little gold-digging town which dates back to the turn of the century. Just beyond Pilgrim's Rest is the attractive *Mount Sheba National Park. Mount Sheba Hotel; 25 rms; Tel. 013/768-12 41; Fax 768-12 48; e-mail: msheba@countryescapes.co.za; category 2*

Tzaneen (103/D3)

★At the foot of the Drakensberg Mountains, on the banks of the great Letaba River, lies this lovely colourful town. The name *Tzaneen* comes from the Hottentot language and means 'in a basket'. This describes the valley in which Tzaneen is located, surrounded by beautiful countryside. The farmers here produce wood, cotton and tropical fruit. Quite close by is ☙*World View* from where the spectacular panorama of the Letaba Valley and the Drakensberg Mountains can be admired. 15 km south of Tzaneen in *Agatha* is *The Coach House,* a country hotel which in recent years has appeared on the list of the best hotels in South Africa. *45 rms; Old Coach Rd.; Tel. 015/307-36 41; Fax 307-16 44; category 1*

Flowers, wine and deserts

These routes are marked in green on the map on the inside front cover and in the Road Atlas beginning on page 102

① WINE ROUTES FOR THE CONNOISSEUR

When it comes to wine, South Africa has plenty to offer, even to the connoisseur who is already well-acquainted with all the well-known wine-growing areas. A trip round the Cape certainly promises a few fine glasses. The drive begins in Cape Town on the N 2 and sets off through Somerset West and Sir Lowry's Pass to Grabouw in the Elgin Valley. It then continues through Worcester, Nuy, Robertson and Swellendam and so returns to Cape Town. The round trip (220 km) takes around half a day.

The first sample in *Grabouw* is not made from grapes but from apples! Heinz, the cider apple grower, has been producing the only cider in southern Africa for over thirty years. Visitors should make arrangements for a tasting in advance at the *Apple Museum* on the *Main Rd. (Tel. 021/859-5000)*. A couple of kilometres further on, turn left off Main Road on the R 43 towards *Villiersdorp*. The road takes you through South Africa's largest fruit-producing area. The view is

especially impressive when the fruit trees are in bloom. Continue driving past huge fruit farms into the mountains. From the heights of *Hottentot's Holland Nature Reserve* there is a fantastic view over one of the ten largest reservoirs in the country, the *Theewaterskloofdam*, beside which the road runs almost as far as Villiersdorp.

The wine-growing area really begins at *Villiersdorp*. The eighty farmers in this region supply the co-operative. The wines can be sampled and bought at the *Kelkiewyn Farmstall (Main Rd.)* The R43 then takes you on to *Worcester*. This town may not be as well-known as Paarl or Stellenbosch, but it is situated in the largest wine-growing area in South Africa. The *Kleinplasie Open Air Living Museum* illustrates how the early pioneers and farmers lived and worked. The buildings are authentic replicas of existing houses from all over the Cape region. *(Mon–Sat 9 am–4.30 pm, Sun 10.30 am–4.30 pm).* Self-catering accommodation is available here, *8 rms; Tel.*

023/342-22 25; category 3. One of these buildings houses the Information Office for the Worcester Wine Route which was formed through collaboration between 24 co-operatives, three wine estates and two brandy cellars *(Tel. 023/342-87 10).* The museum is located a little out of town on the R 60 towards *Robertson* which is where the route goes next. After 15 km turn left towards *Nuy.* Here you can find some really excellent wines, and a very unusual guest house, the *Nuy Valley.* The guest house includes a country restaurant, very pleasant guest rooms and the Conradie family also offers overnight accommodation in the old cement wine tanks on their farm. *(14 rms; Tel. 023/342-12 58, Fax 347-13 56; category 3).* A few kilometres further on along the R 60 is the beginning of *Robertson Valley,* the valley of wine and roses. The first wine co-operative you will reach here is *Rooiberg (Tel. 023/6 26-16 63),* a personal tip for very good, reasonably-priced wine: the Rooi Jerepiko is particularly to be recommended. It is a dessert wine made from pinotage grapes, a variety which is only found in South Africa. The *Oude Fontein Restaurant* on the edge of *Robertson* serves good food and also has an excellent wine menu which focuses on local wines *(Corner of Reitz St. & Adderley St.; Tel. 023/6 26-41 17; category 3).* Almost all the top wine estates on the Robertson Wine Route are on the R 317 which passes through *Bonnievale* and then rejoins the R 60. At the junction with the N 2, which goes either

to Cape Town or to the Garden Route, is *Swellendam,* one of the prettiest historic villages in South Africa. It was founded in 1745 and is the third oldest settlement on the Cape. One of the old houses is now the Tourist Information Bureau *(Oefeningshuis, 36 Voortrekker St.; Tel. 0291/4 27-70).* The *Drostdy Museum* in *Drostdy St.* is one of the most interesting of its kind in the country. It is an open-air museum which comprises several very impressive buildings which were erected between the middle and the end of the 18th century. This was the heyday of the little trade centre of Swellendam. There is an extensive collection of Cape Dutch furniture in the museum. There is an old working water mill *(Mon–Sat 9 am–4 pm).* In Swellendam the choice of pleasant accommodation is wide. The *Klippe Rivier Country House (Tel. 028/514-33 41; Fax 514-33 37; category 2)* is especially recommended. This historic Cape farmhouse is located a little out of the town on the R 60.

② A TRIP INTO FLORAL WONDERLAND

 Between August and October, millions of wild flowers bloom in the west of the Cape Province. They form carpets of all the colours of the rainbow which begin in Darling and extend almost as far as Springbok. The area is called Namaqualand and the flowers Namaqualand daisies. This drive takes you on a half-day trip through this floral wonderland. However, it is worth allowing more time for it as there is lots to see on the 300 km stretch from Cape Town to Nieuwoudtville.

The route starts off on the N 7. Continue until the exit at *Malmesbury*. Turn left here towards *Darling*, a town particularly beloved of the Capetonians. In recent years it has become even more popular, since Pieter Dirk-Uys, South Africa's best cabaret artist, opened his theatre here. During the years of apartheid he satirised the government playing a character called Evita's Bezuidenhout. The theatre and a restaurant are housed in the old village station. The theatre is called *Evita se Peron,* which is Afrikaans for Evita's platform. *(Tel. 022/492-28 31; category 3).* There are many artists and potters living in Darling. The work they produce is exhibited in the *Darling Museum (daily 9 am–1 pm, 2 pm-4 pm). Corner of Pastorie and Hill St. Zum Schatzi* is an excellent German restaurant in *Long St. (Tel. 022/ 492-30 95; category 3).* The best B & B is *Parrots Guest House (5 rms; Tel. 022/492-34 30; category 3).* From Darling take R 307 and then R 45 to *Hopefield.* Be sure to have a look at the *Fossil Museum (Mon–Fri 9 am–4 pm, Sat 10 am–12 pm)* in Main Rd.

Just beyond the village, on the way to *Velddrift* is *Kersefontein.* This is the best opportunity you will have to stay on a Cape Dutch estate. It has been in the Melck family since it was built, three hundred years ago *(Tel. & Fax 022/783-08 50; category 2).* Velddrift is situated in a spectacular setting at the point where the Berg River flows into the Atlantic Ocean. Don't leave the town without seeing the West Coast Gallery. Works by local artists are exhibited here, as well as interesting items made from

sea salt and sea grass, such as soap, spices and handicrafts. The R 399 takes you back to N 7. From there the trip continues northwards as far as *Clanwilliam.* Go through the town and then drive another 36 km on R 364. Here you will see the sign for *Bushman's Kloof* . It is now only another 8 km to a very special hotel with its own game reserve. This private reserve at the foot of the Cedarberg Mountain boasts 140 species of birds and all the wild animals found in the region (from mountain zebras to gemsbok and wild cats). In addition, this is also the site of 125 Bushman paintings, some of which are very well-preserved. Most of them depict people and animals *(Bushman's Kloof Hotel; Tel. 027/4 82-26 27; Fax 4 82-10 11; category 1).* R 363 takes you from here to R 27. Turn left in the direction of *Niewoudtville.* There is an impressive view of the floral splendour from the plateau of the Bokkeveld Mountain. Overnight accommodation is available at the *Van Zijl Guest Houses and Restaurant, 8 rms; Tel. 027/2 68-15 35; Fax 2 68-14 26; category 3.* The route continues through *Vanrhynsdorp* where it rejoins N 7 which either takes you back towards Cape Town or further on towards Namibia.

③ THROUGH SOUTH AFRICA ON A LUXURY TRAIN

 If you want to travel in elegance and style through the Cape countryside, then book a trip with Rovos Rail. One route takes you from Pretoria to Cape Town. For 48 hours you can relax in the comfort of a

luxury train and enjoy 1,600 km of the Karoo landscape.

Saturday afternoon in Pretoria railway station: through the impressive building erected by Herbert Baker in 1920 come the delicate strains of a string quartet. Elegantly-dressed people are gathering on one of the platforms. Champagne is served. Rohan Vos welcomes the passengers to his railway. It is the most luxurious railway line in the world. He recounts how he became interested in old railways as a child and how his dream became reality with Rovos Rail. The story continues, telling how he travelled throughout the country looking for old locomotives and carriages. The locomotive which is to pull the train on the first part of its journey today is called the 'Pride of Africa'.

Rovos Rail provides two different kinds of accommodation. There are the Royal Suites which are around 16 m^2 and include a double bed and a sitting area. In the bathroom all the old fittings have been retained and combined with the modern. Each of these suites takes up half a carriage. The De Luxe Suites are a little smaller at 11 m^2. Once the train has departed, the passengers assemble in carriage no. 226, the 'Observation and Bar Car'. Its windows have been enlarged and part of the carriage is completely glazed to afford a better view. Two hours later the train arrives in *Johannesburg (page 81-85)*. After a short stop here the journey continues. At 8 pm dinner is served. Most of the passengers dress for dinner as it seems appropriate in the atmosphere of the train. There are only ever as many passengers as can be seated in the dining car so that there is always only one sitting for meals. The dishes are exquisite and accompanied by wonderful South African wines. On Sunday morning breakfast is served in the dining car at 8 am. At 10 am the train arrives in *Kimberley (page 52-54)*, where the passengers are invited to go on a tour of the city. On their return it is already lunch-time and the train resumes its journey. The next stop is not for more than 700 km. A large part of the trip is through the *Karoo*. On Monday morning the train stops in *Matjesfontein* for breakfast. This is a little town on the edge of the Karoo. Originally it was no more than a railway station for the farmers of the region. But in 1876 Douglas Logan, a Scot with TB, discovered the healing effect of the dry climate here. For a few decades, Logan transformed the village into a thriving health resort. Matjesfontein looks today much as it would have done in Logan's time.

Breakfast is served in the historic Lord Milner Hotel. Afterwards you can go for a stroll through the little village and then the journey continues. After two hours the landscape begins to change as the train reaches the fertile *Cape*. What a feast for the eyes after the semi-desert land of the Karoo! Past Cape Dutch farm houses surrounded by orchards and vineyards, the party approaches *Cape Town (page 37-43)*. The journey finally comes to an end at 6 pm at Cape Town station. *For information on prices and booking see page 96.*

Practical information

Important addresses and useful information for your visit to South Africa

AMERICAN & BRITISH ENGLISH

The Marco Polo travel guides are written in British English. In North America, certain terms and usages deviate from British usage. Some of the more frequently encountered examples are:
baggage for luggage, billion for milliard, cab for taxi, car rental for car hire, drugstore for chemist's, fall for autumn, first floor for groundfloor, freeway/highway for motorway, gas(oline) for petrol, railroad for railway, restroom for toilet/lavatory, streetcar for tram, subway for underground/tube, toll-free numbers for freephone numbers, trailer for caravan, trunk for boot, vacation for holidays, wait staff for waiting staff (in restaurants etc.), zip code for postal code.

BARS

The bars, even in hotels, are not always open to women. However, most hotels also have a Ladies Bar.

BED & BREAKFAST

Private accommodation is available all over the country. And more establishments are opening every day. The choice is endless; from simple farm houses to grand estates. Most of the B&Bs have joined to form the Bed and Breakfast Collection. Their catalogue is available from South African travel agents. *Number for central reservations: 011/880-3414; Fax 788-4802.*

CAMPING

South Africa's climate is ideal for campers. There are excellent camp sites in all towns, on beaches and in nature reserves and game parks. *Information Tel. 011/789-3202*

CAR RENTAL

Car rental is available in every town and prices are reasonable. There are often special offers for tourists. The main car rental firms are *Avis Tel. 08000/211-11, Budget Tel. 08000/166-22* and *Imperial Car/Hertz Tel. 08002/102-27.* Visitors looking for something cheaper can rent a car from *Rent a Wreck.* Despite the name, the cars are not just fit for the scrap heap! *Tel. 011/402-7043.* The minimum age to rent a car is 23. An international driving licence is also required.

COMPUTICKET

A central reservation system for tickets for cinema, opera, theatre and other events. Advanced booking offices can be found in department stores, shopping centres and arcades in all large towns.

CONSULATES

British High Commission
255 Hill Street, Pretoria 0002; Tel. 12/483-12 00; Fax 483-13 02; e-mail: bhc@icon.co.za; Internet: www.britain.org.za

British Consulate General
15th Floor, Southern Life Centre, 8 Riebeeck St., Cape Town 8000; Tel. 21/425-36 70; Fax 425-14 27.
Consulates in:
Durban, East London, Johannesburg and Port Elizabeth.

Canadian High Commission
1103 Arcadia St., Hatfield 0083, Pretoria; Tel. 12/422-30 00; Fax 422-30 52: Internet: www.canada.co.za

Embassy of the United States
877 Pretorius St.; Arcadia 0003; Tel. 12/342-10 48; Fax 342-22 99; e-mail: mjnpretoria@mhs.cstat.co.za; Internet: www.usia.gov/abtusia/posts/SF1/wwwhmain.html.
Consulates in: Cape Town, Durban and Johannesburg.

in Great Britain:
South African Consulate
15 Whitehall, London, W1A 2DD; Tel. 0171/92 5-89 00; Fax 930-15 10

in Canada:
High Commission of the Republic of South Africa
15 Sussex Dr., Ottawa, Ontario, K1M 1M8; Tel. 613/744-03 30; Fax 741-16 39; e-mail: safrica@sympatico.ca; Internet: www.docuweb.ca/SouthAfrica
Consulates in: Montreal and Toronto.

in the United States:
Embassy of the Republic of South Africa
3051 Massachusetts Ave., NW, Washington, DC 20008; Tel. 202/232-4400; Fax 265 16 07; e-mail: safrica@southafrica.net; Internet: www.southafrica.net. Consulates in: Chicago, Los Angeles and New York

CUSTOMS

The following goods may be imported into South Africa by passengers over 18 years of age without incurring customs duty: 400 cigarettes and 50 cigars and 250 g of tobacco; 1 litre of spirits and 2 litres of wine; 50 ml of perfume and 250 ml of eau de toilette; gifts up to a value of 1,250 R per person. Note: there is a flat rate duty of 20% on gifts in excess of 1,250 up to 10,000 R. Protected plants and animals or derivative products may not be imported.

DRIVING

In South Africa cars may not be driven without *third party insurance* which only covers injuries to persons. Speed limit in built-up areas is 60 km/h, on open roads 100 km/h, on highways 120 km/h. There are about 84,000 kilometres of tarred roads and a further 163,000 km of roads which are not paved. Driving is on the left. Strictly no drinking and driving.

Accidents are only recorded by the police if injuries to persons are involved. In all other cases the drivers simply exchange addresses and both report the accident at a police station. It is not essential to carry a driving licence when driving, it is sufficient to take it to the police within 24 hours, if required. The Automobile Association (AA) has branches throughout the country. *Tel. 011/ 403-5700*

GOLF

Information from Golf Union in Johannesburg, *Tel. 011/ 640-3714*

HEALTH

Visitors to the Kruger Park and the adjoining game reserves are advised to take preventative measures against malaria. Malaria tablets are available from chemists in South Africa and a prescription is not required. Anyone travelling to South Africa from a yellow fever zone must be able to prove that they have been immunised against it.

As there is no state health service in South Africa, visitors must pay for treatment and medication themselves and are strongly advised to take out international medical insurance. Doctors can be found in the phone book under *Medical*. Chemists are found under *Chemist* or *Pharmacy*.

HOTELS

Special offers are almost always available, especially from the major chains, such as *Protea, Southern Sun, Holiday Inn* and *Sun International* (very attractive grounds).

INFORMATION

South African Tourism Board (satour)
442 Rigel Avenue South, Erasmusrand, Pretoria 0181, South Africa;

Tel. 12/3 47-06 00; Fax 347-87 53; e-mail: satour@icon.co.za

in the United Kingdom
South African High Commission, South Africa House, Trafalgar Square, London, WC2N 5DP; Tel. 0171/ 930-48 88 or 0891/441-100 (visa, etc.); Fax 0171/ 451 72 84; e-mail: london@businesssouthafrica.com

South African Tourism Board (SA-TOUR), 5-6 Alt Grove, London, SW19 4DZ; Tel. 0181/944-80 80; Fax 0181/944-67 05; e-mail: satour@satbuk.demon.co.uk; www.tourist-offices.org.uk

in the United States
South African Tourism Board (SA-TOUR), Suite 2040, 500 Fifth Avenue, New York, NY 10110; Tel. 212/730-29 29 or 1800/822-53 68 (toll free; USA only); Fax 212/764-19 80; e-mail: satourny@ aol.com; Internet: www.satour.org

in Canada
South African Tourism Board (SA-TOUR), Suite 200, 43 Colbourne St.; Toronto, Ontario, M5E 1E3; Tel. 416/861-87 90; Fax 416/ 861-11 08

MEASURES & WEIGHTS

1 cm	0.39 inch
1 m	1.09 yd (3.28 ft)
1 km	0.62 miles
1 m^2	1.20 yd^2
1 ha	2.47 acres
1 km^2	0.39 mi^2
1 g	0.035 ounces
1 kg	2.21 pounds
British tonne	1016 kg
US ton	907 kg

1 litre is equivalent to 0.22 Imperial gallons and 0.26 US gallons

MONEY

It is illegal to bring more than 50,000 R into South Africa. There are no limits to the amount of foreign currency which may be brought in. Credit cards: Master-Card, American Express, Diners Club and Visa are widely accepted. Check your credit card company for details of merchant acceptability and other services. Travellers cheques: valid at banks, hotels, restaurants and shops. To avoid additional exchange rate charges, visitors are advised to take travellers cheques in pounds sterling.

OPENING TIMES

Banks are open Mon–Fri from 9 am–3.30 pm and Sat from 8.30 am–11 pm. Shops: Mon–Fri, 8.30 am–5 pm and Sat 8.30 am–1 pm. Post offices: Mon–Fri 8.30 am–4.30 pm, Sat 8 am–12 pm.

PASSPORT & VISA

Visitors from the UK, USA and Canada do not need a visa but must have a return ticket. Passports valid for at least 6 months beyond the date of departure from South Africa are required by all. Holders of visitors' visas cannot take up employment in South Africa. Tourists can have the VAT reimbursed at the airports in Johannesburg, Durban and Cape Town. But since many visitors have the same idea, you should allow plenty of time for this. *Information Tel. 011/484-75 30; Fax 484-29 52*

PHOTOGRAPHY

Military sites, police stations and prisons may not be photographed.

RAILWAYS

The only really good, reliable train services are those provided by the *Blue Train* and *Rovos Rail.*
The rest are all slow, often fairly uncomfortable and generally not to be recommended.

The journey with the Blue Train takes you from Cape Town to Pretoria with a stop in Johannesburg in around 24 hours. The train starts almost silently and with very little vibration, slowly at first, from the green coastal region. The narrow track winds its way through fertile farmland and then goes straight through the Karoo. From the window, passengers can look out at the diamond fields. Eventually, the high plateau of the north is reached. Passengers can spend the hours of their journey entirely as they please; either in the salon, in the elegant dining car or in their compartment. The food is good and the wine menu exquisite. The choice of accommodation ranges from rather narrow single compartments to large suites, complete with bathroom and salon. The service is excellent. Where else can you travel by train and find a bar of chocolate laid on your bed? The atmosphere is one of tradition, after all, train travel has existed since 1901. Passengers are expected to dress up for dinner. The train goes in both directions on Mon, Wed and Fri. It costs over 1,000 R for a single ticket in a single compartment and over 8,000 for a return ticket in a luxury suite. *Reservations in Johannesburg, Tel. 011/774-44 69. Further information on rail travel from South African Railways (SPOOR-NET); Website: www.spoornet.co.za*

The golden age of steam and luxury rail travel has also been brought back to life by *Rovos Rail*, in the middle of the African bush. The elaborately renovated Rovos Line has eight 1920s carriages which are pulled by three locomotives, dating from 1893, 1926 and 1938. They operate on several different routes. The owner spent years in the search for locomotives and carriages and then went to great pains to restore them. 40 passengers can travel on the trains at any one time and are looked after by a staff of 14. The excellent food is prepared in a 1924 kitchen wagon. The cabins, salons and dining car are decorated in the style of the turn of the century, with all attention to comfort. Rovos Rail also offers a steam train safari which sets off on a journey of 1,000 km from Pretoria, through Mpumalanga to Graskop. The passengers feel as if they have stepped back in time to the age of the adventurers, pioneers, gold-diggers and elephant hunters. There are also trips going to Cape Town, the Victoria Falls or to the Garden Route. Once a year Rovos Rail offers to make the 6,000-km trip to Dar es Salaam – a remarkable experience not just for the railway buff. (see also Routes in South Africa page 91). *The cost of the trips in South Africa is between 2,000 and 6,000 rand. Reservations on Tel. 12/323-60 52; Fax 323-08 43.*

Safari by car in Kruger Park

SAFARIS

Safaris are available to suit every taste and every pocket. *Information on SATSA (Southern African Tourism & Safari Ass.), Tel. 011/883-9103; Fax 883-9002.* Special tip: three hours drive from Johannesburg is *Lindbergh Lodge.* Many famous visitors have stayed the night at the Lindberghs' elegant country house, including Cecil Rhodes. The estate is situated in a game park which is comparable only to the Serengeti. Visitors can go on safari by balloon here and fly almost silently above large herds of wildebeest, giraffes, kudu and zebras. *17 rms; Wolmaransstad; Tel. 018/596-20 41; Fax 596-2048; e-mail: lindberg@iaafrica.com; category 1 and 2*

TELEPHONES

With the exception of rural areas, the telephone network is fully automatic, with direct dialling to most places in the world. Post offices will make international calls which cannot usually be made from public telephones. *International code for the UK: 00 44 International code for the US: 00 1 International code for Canada: 00 1 International code for South Africa: 00 27*

Mobile phones can be hired at the airports.
Directory enquiries: 10 23 International dir. enquiries: 19 23

Power supply is 220 Volts a/c, 50 Hz. An adaptor plug which is only available in South Africa is required to connect two-pin plugs. Hotels will supply an adaptor.

TIME DIFFERENCES

During European Summer Time: same time; in winter: one hour ahead. US Eastern Standard Time: + 7. Greenwich Mean Time: + 2.

WILD WATER RAFTING

Dinghy or canoe trips are offered on the Tugela, Orange and Vaal Rivers. They generally last for between one and six days. Information is available from *River & Safaris; Tel. 011/803-97 75; Fax 803-96 03.*

WEATHER IN JOHANNESBURG
Seasonal averages

Daytime temperatures in °C/F

Jan	Feb	Mar	Apr	May	June	July	Aug	Sept	Oct	Nov	Dec
26/79	25/77	24/75	22/72	19/66	17/63	17/63	20/68	23/73	25/77	25/77	26/79

Night-time temperatures in °C/F

Jan	Feb	Mar	Apr	May	June	July	Aug	Sept	Oct	Nov	Dec
15/59	14/57	13/55	10/50	6/43	4/39	4/39	6/43	9/48	12/54	13/55	14/57

Sunshine: hours per day

Jan	Feb	Mar	Apr	May	June	July	Aug	Sept	Oct	Nov	Dec
8	8	7	8	9	9	9	10	9	9	9	9

Rainfall: days per month

Jan	Feb	Mar	Apr	May	June	July	Aug	Sept	Oct	Nov	Dec
13	9	8	7	3	1	0	1	2	8	11	12

Do's and don'ts

How to avoid some of the traps and pitfalls that face the unwary traveller in South Africa

Safety
Many people on holiday enjoy going for a stroll round the block after dinner. This is not recommended in the larger cities of South Africa. It is too dangerous. In Johannesburg drivers are no longer required to stop at red lights when travelling at night as there have recently been many cases of muggings. It is advisable to lock the car from the inside when driving in the city. When going to a restaurant, ask about the location of the carpark and how far away it is from the restaurant.

It is usually quite safe to go for a walk along the sea front. However, visitors to Table Mountain who wish to go to the more isolated view points off the beaten track, should make sure they do not take all their cash with them. Even during the day, try to carry money and cameras so that they are inconspicuous and always lock up valuables in the hotel safe.

The telephone number for emergencies is: *101 11.*

Highways
Visitors from abroad may be surprised to find that it is quite common for pedestrians and dogs to cross the highway. Be aware of this, especially in and around the townships. Look out for cyclists and joggers, too. Drivers should also be aware that horses, cows and sheep often graze on the central reservations of highways.

Beggars
Compared to other countries in Africa, there are relatively few beggars in South Africa. However, it is not unusual in the larger towns for children to come up to cars at traffic lights or as they are being parked. Try not to give them any money, regardless of how heart-rending it may be. The children are usually members of organised gangs and the money is taken away from them by the adults. However, you can't go wrong by giving them sweets or an apple. Nevertheless, it is advisable to drive with the car doors locked when in the larger towns and cities.

Feeding animals
Feeding animals is prohibited in all the game parks. The baboons which often live near roads and around service stations should not (and indeed may not) be fed either. Many of them have lost their natural fear of humans. When a car stops they often

climb on to the roof and as soon as one of the doors is opened, they come and sit in the car and look for anything edible. They love to steal anything which is not sewn on or fastened down. It has happened that they have made off with a brief case full of papers, never to be seen again.

Don't feed the animals in the game parks

Queue jumping

Queuing etiquette is important in South Africa. Regardless of what you are waiting for, whether it be a bus, cinema tickets or in the bank, queue jumping is considered to be impolite.

Hitch-hikers

Because of the unreliable public transport system, there are many people who stand at the edge of the road, waiting for a ride. Still, it is important to be wary. South Africans are always ready to help and no-one waits for long. However, it is difficult for tourists to judge when and where it is wise to offer a lift and whom it is safe to pick up.

Zebra crossings

In South Africa, and especially in Cape Town, visitors should not take it for granted that drivers will take any notice of zebra crossings. Similarly, as a driver, you should not assume that pedestrians will stop at a red light. Capetonians simply rely on the fact that drivers will always brake.

Work ethic

A Johannesburg businessman describes his colleagues in Cape Town: each day anyone who can manage it disappears for lunch between the hours of 11 am and 4 pm. Every Wednesday afternoon the Capetonians have an extremely important meeting on the golf course which absolutely must not be missed. On Fridays every attempt is made to leave the office before lunch-time and to stretch the lunch break out until Monday (at the very earliest!). This state of affairs is fine for the summer months between November and April. However, December and January are particularly hard months. For one thing it is very hot and for another it is the holiday season. Apart from that, it is hardly worth going back to work in between all the bank holidays and Christmas etc. Well, unless you're a swimming instructor, that is.

Road Atlas of South Africa

*Please refer to back cover for an overview
of this Road Atlas*

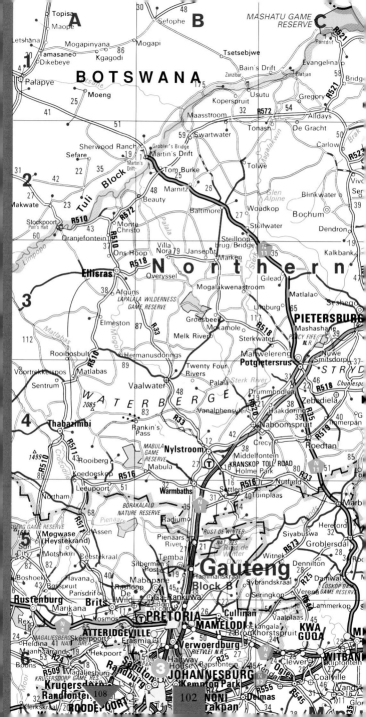

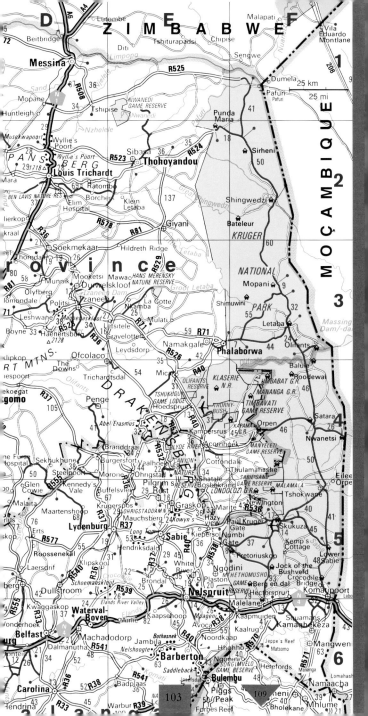

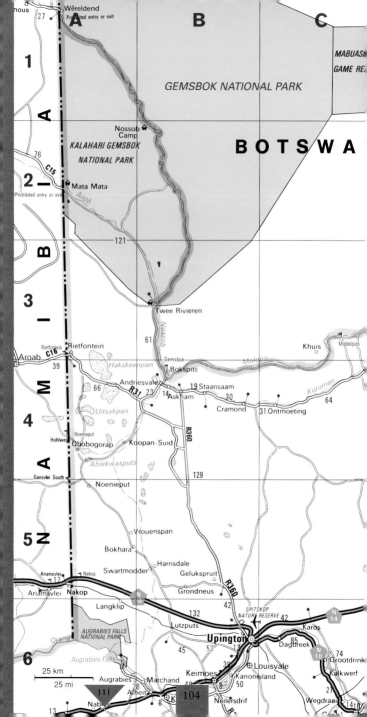

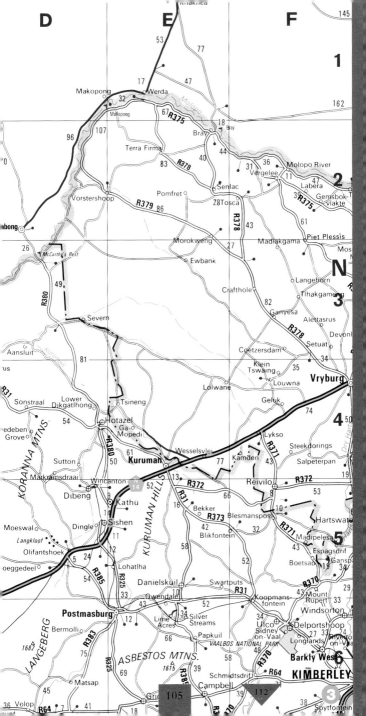

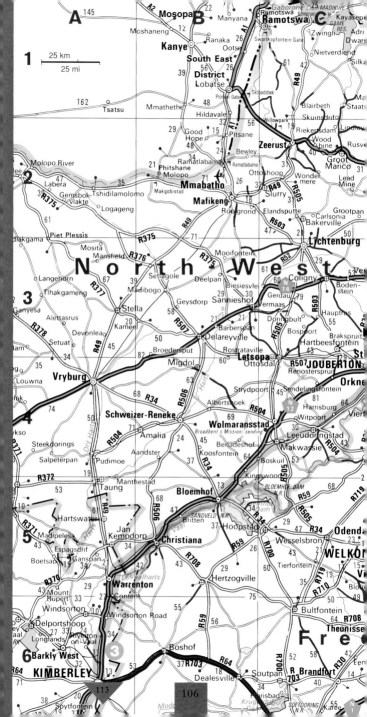

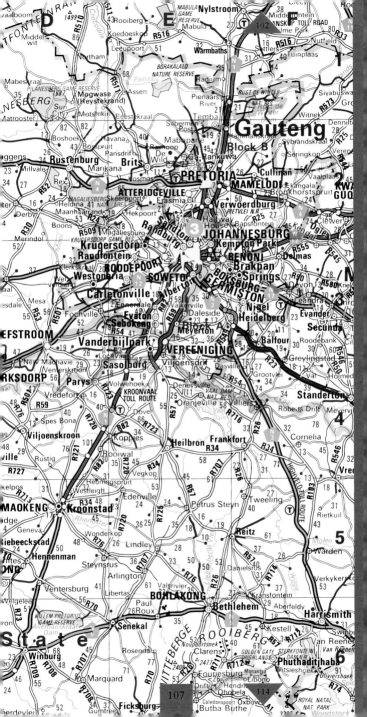

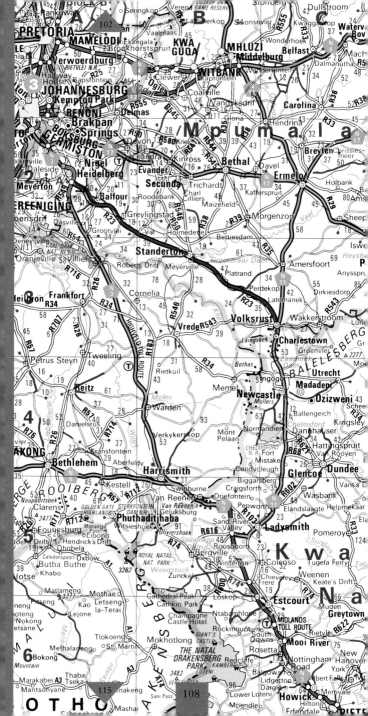

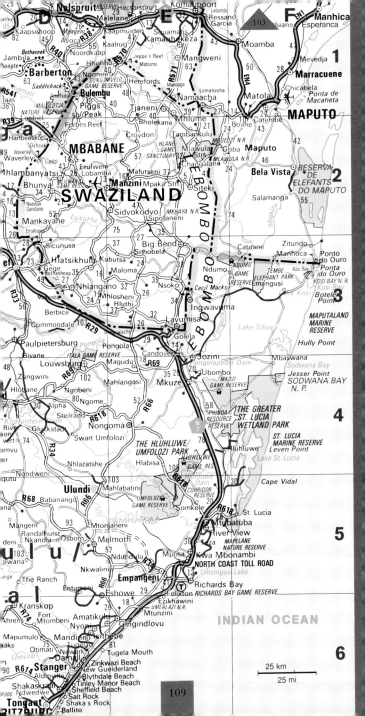

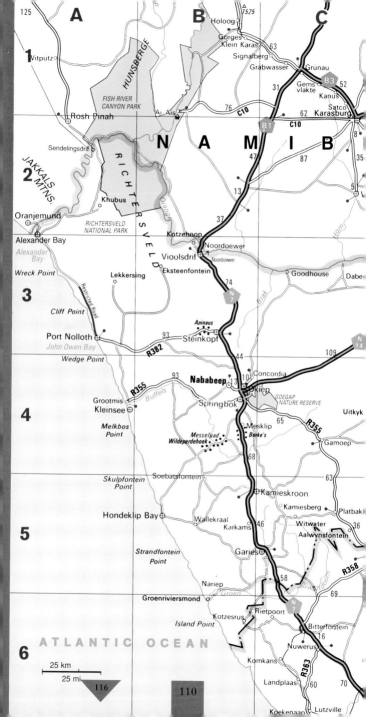

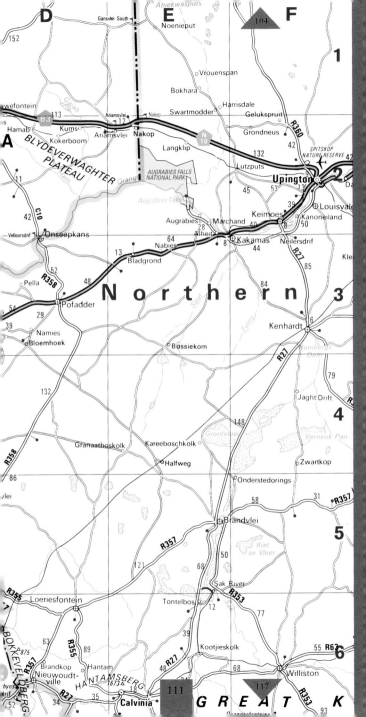

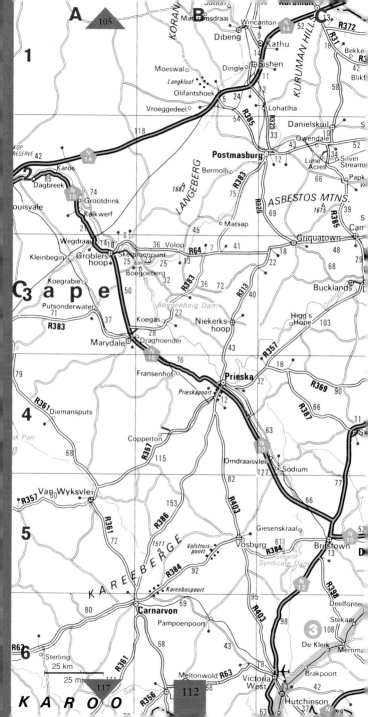

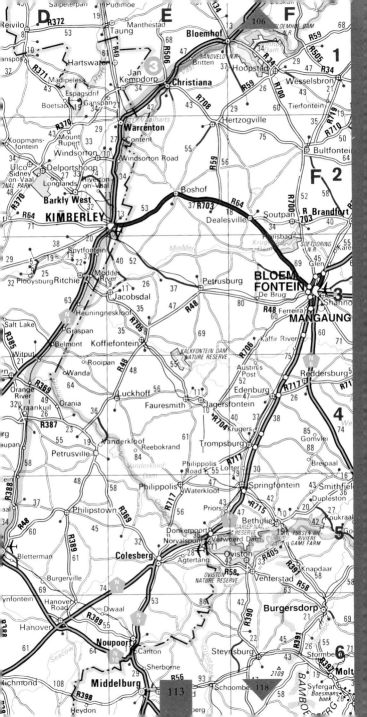

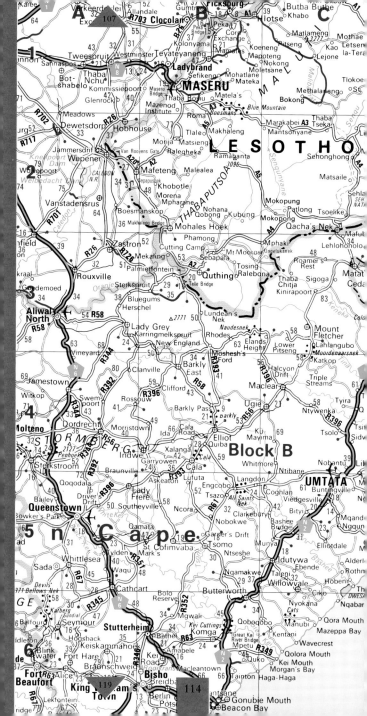

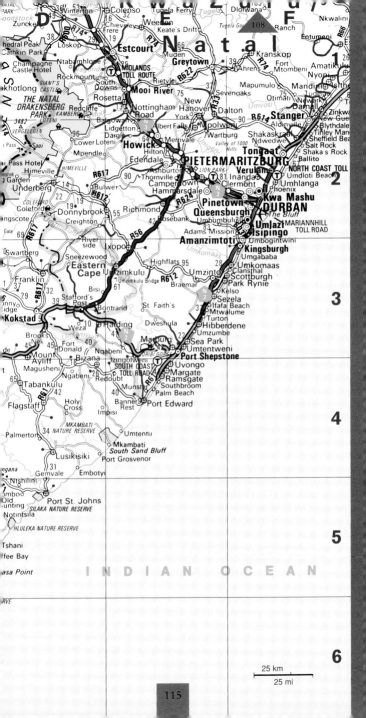

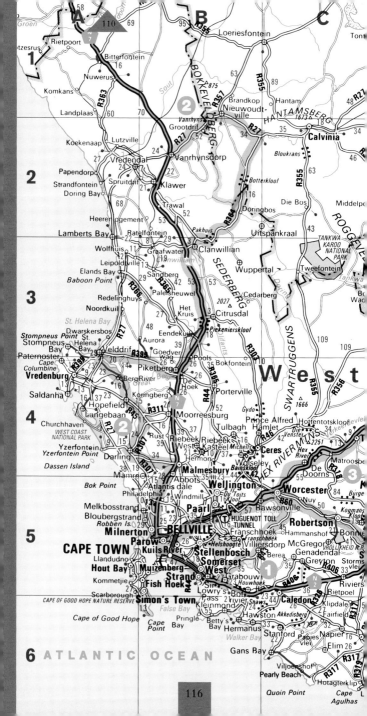

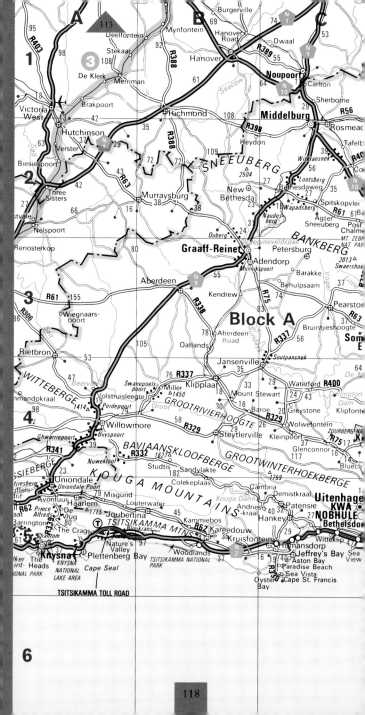

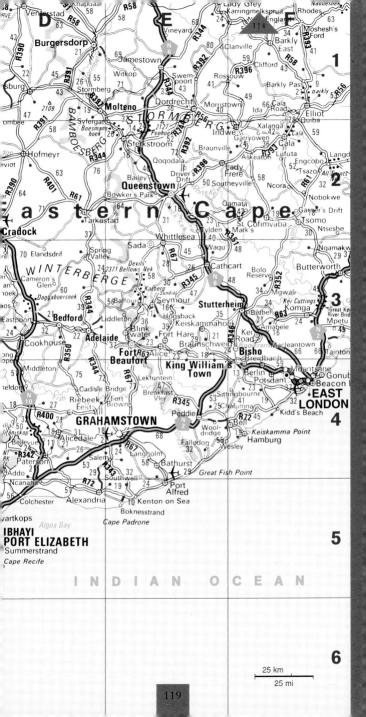

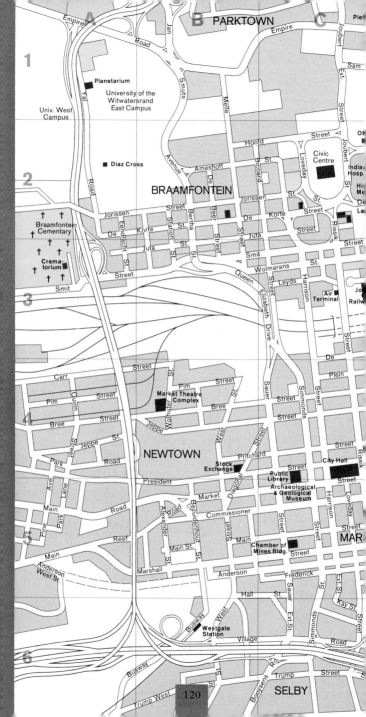

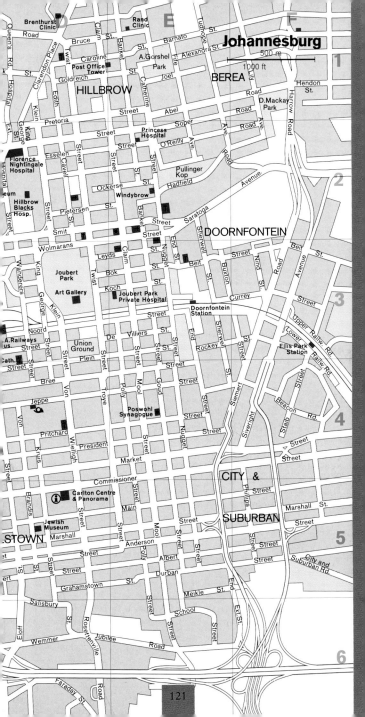

Johannesburg

500 m / 1000 ft

BEREA

HILLBROW

DOORNFONTEIN

CITY & SUBURBAN

Brenthurst Clinic
Rand Clinic
Post Office Tower
Florence Nightingale Hospital
Hillbrow Blacks Hosp.
Princess Hospital
Windybrow
Pullinger Kop
Joubert Park
Art Gallery
Joubert Park Private Hospital
Doornfontein Station
Union Ground
Ellis Park Station
S.A.Railways us.
Jeppe
Poswohl Synagogue
Carlton Centre & Panorama
Jewish Museum
D.Mackay Park

Queen's Rd.
Clarendon Place
Twist
Bruce St.
Clam St.
Banket St.
Caroline
Goldreich
Barnato St.
A.Gorshel
Park
Alexandra St.
Tudhope St.
Joel
Catherine
Hendon St.
Harrow Road
Pretoria
Edith
Klein
George St. Ext.
King George St. Ext.
Esselen
Cavell
Abel
Soper
O'Reilly
Road
Road
Road
Road
Hadfield
Ockerse St.
Pietersen St.
Banket Street
Saratoga
Avenue
Smit
Wolmarans
Leyds
Clam St.
Nugget
Beit
Sherwell
Beit
Burton
Nind
Road
Avenue
Avenue
Beit St.
Street
Bok
Koch St.
Twist
Currey
Upper Railw. Rd.
Lower Railw. Rd.
Street
De Villiers St.
End St.
Rockey
Sherwell
Siemert
Staib
Noord Street
King
George
Klein
Plein
Bree
Von
Troye
Mooi
Poly
Gold
Street
Nugget St.
Siemert
Beacon Rd.
Staib
Wanderers
Jeppe
Pritchard
Weiligh
President
Market
Commissioner
Main Street
Mooi
Poly
Nugget
Phillips
Marshall St.
Marshall Street
STOWN
Marshall
Anderson
Albert
Durban
Meikle St.
School
End St.
Ext St.
City and Suburban Rd.
Grahamstown St.
Salisbury
Wemmer
Rosettenville
Jubilee
Road
Eloff
Faraday St.
Krus
Brands

121

ROAD ATLAS LEGEND

○	Hauptstädte und Städte Capitals and cities
⊙	über 50 000 Einwohner over 50 000 population
◎	10 000 - 50 000 Einwohner 10 000 - 50 000 population
⊙	5 000 - 10 000 Einwohner 5 000 - 10 000 population
⊕	500 - 5 000 Einwohner 500 - 5 000 population
○	unter 500 under 500
	Autobahn mit Anschlüssen Freeway with intersections
	Autobahn in Bau Freeway under construction
	Autobahn in Planung Freeway proposed
	Nationalstraße National Route
Ⓣ	Gebührenpflichtige Straße Toll Road
Tarred *Under Construction* *Untarred*	Durchgangsstraße Principal trunk road
	Hauptstraße Main road
	Nebenstraße Secondary road
	Eisenbahn Railway
	Staatsgrenze National boundary
	Provinzgrenze Provincial boundary
33	Entfernung in Kilometern Distance in kilometres
Cala	Bergpaß Mountain pass
	Nationalpark, Tier- und Naturschutzgebiet National park, game and nature reserve
◀ Beitbridge	Grenzkontrolle Border control post
△ 1867	Höhenangabe in Metern Height in metres
✈	Flughafen Airport
R29	Straßennummern Route numbers

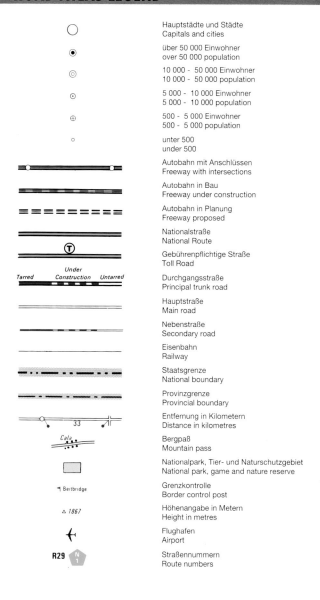

INDEX

This index lists all the main sights, places and game parks mentioned in this guide. Numbers in bold indicate a main entry, italic a photograph.

What do you get for your money?

 The unit of currency is the rand which is equal to 100 cents. There are 1, 2, 5, 10, 20 and 50 cent and 1, 2, and 5 rand coins. There are 5, 10, 20, 50, 100, 200 and 500 rand notes. Inflation in South Africa is high. Rates of exchange differ from day to day — check the newspaper for current exchange rates. Because the exchange rate is continually adjusted, visitors do not suffer the effects of inflation. It is cheaper to change rand in South Africa.

A flight from Johannesburg to Cape Town costs around 750 rand but there are often special offers on night flights and weekend trips. Gas costs are relatively cheap as is the price of a packet of cigarettes. Admission to museums is almost always free. Where admission is charged then it is usually very low and is generally free for children. Cinema tickets cost around 7.50 rand. At the restaurant in Sea Point, a popular holiday suburb of Cape Town, a pizza will cost you 15 rand. For the same price it is possible to get a three-course meal at a hotel in a rural area. A good bottle of table wine costs 7.50 rand in the shop. The admission to the national parks is generally around 11 rand per person, it costs another 11 rand for a car and overnight accommodation costs about 15 rand per person.

US$	Rand	£	Rand	Can$	Rand
1	6.05	1	9.56	1	4.12
2	12.11	2	19.12	2	8.23
3	18.16	3	28.69	3	12.35
4	24.21	4	38.25	4	16.47
5	30.27	5	47.81	5	20.58
10	60.53	10	95.62	10	41.17
15	90.80	15	143.43	15	61.75
20	121.06	20	191.24	20	82.34
25	151.33	25	239.05	25	102.92
30	181.59	30	286.86	30	123.51
40	242.12	40	382.48	40	164.68
50	302.66	50	478.10	50	205.85
60	363.19	60	573.73	60	247.02
70	423.72	70	669.35	70	288.18
80	484.25	80	764.97	80	329.35
90	544.78	90	860.59	90	370.52
100	605.31	100	956.21	100	411.69
200	1,210.62	200	1,912.42	200	823,38
300	1,815.93	300	2,868.62	300	1,235.07
400	2,421.24	400	3,824.83	400	1,646.77
500	3,026.55	500	4,781.04	500	2,058.46
750	4,539.82	750	7,107.56	750	3,087.69
1,000	6,053.10	1,000	9,562.08	1,000	4,116.91